Tales from the Isle of Nodd

by
Duncan Fraser

Published by the Gates of Horn Press, Bishopstone, 2025

Contents

Illustrations

Cover photograph by Duncan Fraser.

Illustrations for The Ogres are Coming, Trouble with the Chickens, The Treasure Hunt, and Dream On by Ruth de Mallet Morgan.

Illustrations for Bruin and the Wolf, Surprise Surprise!, and Bruin in Shadowland by Duncan Fraser.

The Ogres Are Coming

The queen swept into the room with a shriek that made the potted plants quiver to their roots.

"Clovis!"

Her husband, the king, to whom this was addressed, paused with his spoon over the egg which he was just about to crack. Their children, the twins Bruin and Karlo, looked up with their mouths open and full of food. It was not a pretty sight. The cats, too many to name, let out a brief, single sigh, then returned to their snoozing.

"One moment, Clotilde, my dear," said Clovis. "The egg."

"The egg!" cried the queen. "The EGG! Eggs must wait a moment. Eggs are nothing compared to this."

The spoon wavered uncertainly for a second. A minute's delay and the egg would be ruined, the yolk would begin to go dry at the edges and turn a dull cream colour instead of being soft and golden all the way through. This could set the day off to a very bad start and cast a cloud over all that followed. The king, you see, took breakfast very seriously.

On the other hand, he thought to himself, Clotilde is a sensible person, someone who understands the importance of breakfast. Whatever it is that has upset her must be, as she says, more important than eggs.

All that, and more, can pass through a mind in much less time than it takes for a spoon to wave three times over an uncracked egg-shell. Clovis laid his spoon aside.

"What is it, my dear?"

*   *   *

Clotilde and Clovis were queen and king of the island of Nodd. It was a peaceful, law-abiding land where little happened to disturb people's lives beyond the odd sheep straying into a garden and eating all the brussels sprouts. But there were always plenty of sprouts to go round, so the owners of the offending sheep would simply repay the losses from their own garden and harmony would be restored once more.

It is true, there were some odd customs in Nodd, one of the oddest being that the queen and king took it in turns to rule, each having one day on, and the next off. This custom came about because, many monarchs back, the king and his wife had twins, a boy and a girl, and when their father died neither had married, so they both had an equal claim to the thone. After much debate it was therefore decided that they would inherit half the throne each, and since cutting a throne in half would have made a rather uncomfortable seat, they took it in turns to sit on it – one on one day and the other on the next. The king then died without having had any children, and the queen had one, a daughter, who married before inheriting the throne and decided to continue this custom of the dual monarchy when she did so.

When Clovis married, he chose, by pure chance, a partner who was born on the very same day as he was, so they, too, were in a sense twins, albeit in age only.

There was. as you will now understand, rather a habit of being a twin in this family.

On this particular day, it was Clotilde's turn to rule, so Clovis thought that maybe something important had happened in the ruling department.

*   *   *

"I've got the most dreadful news – a family of ogres has bought the old palace next door and they are moving in this very day."

"Ogres ... ogres...," mused the king. "But we don't have any ogres in Nodd – they all live in Fuliginea. It's miles away … over there …" He waved his hand towards the window. His geography was a little vague.

"Egg-sactly," replied Clotilde (and Clovis thought wistfully for a moment about his lost breakfast). "Miles away" (the king was, too) "and I don't see why they can't stay there, with" – and here she cast a meaningful glance at the children who, luckily, were busy again with boiled eggs and bread soldiers – "their horrible habits."

"Ogres ... the habits of ogres ..." Then he realised what his wife was getting at. "Great cornflakes! I see what you mean, my dear. But what can we do?"

"We must stop them, of course. There won't be a child left in the house if we don't. Oh!" she wailed, and ran to clutch her children to her, "all my pretty ones ..."

"Now, now, Clotilde," said the king, "don't get upset. Sit down and let's think about this."

He pushed a cat off her chair and moved the coffee pot towards her. "Have you had a proper breakfast?"

"Oh, I can't think of breakfast at the moment," sobbed the queen. "We must do something."

She let go of the children, who were beginning to wriggle. "You can go and play, you two – your father and I have something important to talk about – but don't go anywhere near the old palace. You must stay in the garden – do you hear?"

"Yes, mother," came the reply as the twins rushed out into the sunshine, but they were far too happy to take any notice of what she had said.

*   *   *

The queen sent an e-mail requesting one of the Bailiffs of the Tomes to attend the royal presence. This sounds very grand, but all it meant was that the three of them – queen, king and Bailiff – would sit in big comfy chairs and have a chat over a cup of tea.

The Bailiffs looked after the tomes (or books) that contained all the laws and the history of the Isle of Nodd, but Bailiff Right had not actually brought any of them with her. She did not need to as she knew them all off by heart. In fact, it was so long since anyone had actually read them that nobody knew exactly where the tomes were any more. It was even rumoured that they were lost, but nobody cared at all since the Bailiffs had remarkable memories – they never ever went into a room and forgot what they had gone in there for.

There were two Bailiffs and, like the king and queen, they took it in turns to be on duty. Unlike the king and queen, however, both the Bailiffs were women and they had only one good eye each. The one who had responded to the royal request on this occasion was blind in her left eye but had perfect sight in her right eye, and so was called Bailiff Right. Her partner was blind in her right eye but had perfect sight in her left and so was known as Bailiff Left. Altogether though, they had a perfectly good pair of eyes between them, and they got along very well like that. Luckily, they did not need spectacles.

"Well, Bailiff," said the queen, "we have asked you here to find out if there are any laws in Nodd which say that ogres are not allowed to live here."

The Bailiff fixed her eye on her toes for a long while, as though the laws were written on them. At last she breathed in and said, very definitely, "no."

"Are there any laws about ogres?" asked Clotilde.

Again the Bailiff studied her toes (and during the pause we might note that the Bailiff wore no shoes, though in this respect she was not in any way strange, since nobody on Nodd wore shoes).

"Yes," she replied eventually. "They may not carry bags of soot through the streets of any city, town, village, hamlet, or thorpe, nor on any highway, road, track or pathway between or leading to or from any of the aforesaid cities, towns, villages, hamlets or thorpes during the hours of darkness, except on Midsummer's Night, and even then only by special permission of the Monarch of the Day ruling on Midsummer's Eve."

"Oh dear!" said the king. "That's awful."

"Why so, my dear?" asked the queen, somewhat puzzled by his response.

"Because it means that they can carry bags of soot wherever they like during daylight," replied Clovis.

"Ah, just so," said his wife and, realising immediately what Clovis's next point would be, added, "which in turn means they must be allowed to live here in order to carry the bags of soot around in the first place."

"Egg-sactly," said the king.

"But, Bailiff," he continued, "is that the only law concerning ogres in the tomes?"

"I'm afraid it is, king," replied the Bailiff, though not without a further lengthy study of her toes.

9

"But how did such a law come into existence?" asked Clotilde, much puzzled. "I have never heard, in all my life, from any one of my relations, not even my ancient Great-Grandmother, who lived to be ninety-three years old, of an ogre living in Nodd."

"It is indeed a very old law," said the Bailiff, "which is why I had to go through nearly all my toes to get to it, and the circumstances were somewhat peculiar.

"There were," she continued, "about a hundred and fifty years ago, many ogres on our island, and they lived, it appears, very peaceably with their neighbours, the native Noddians. They were, however, much given to a sport called Soot Hurling, in which the competitors would hurl bags of soot of a certain size – the size depending on the age and strength of the hurler – not with the aim of hurling them further than anyone else, but of spreading the soot on the bag's contact with the ground over a greater area than anyone else. Now the Noddians are, as you well know, very clean and tidy people, and this sport made many of them feel more than a little uneasy on account of the mess that it created. It was not so much the mess on the fields of play – they had no objection to that, as they considered soot on the playing field to be 'something in the right place', and of course the

Noddian believes very sensibly that dirt is simply 'something in the wrong place.' No, this uneasiness was purely on account of the occasional and inevitable accidents that took place in the streets when, as it might be, ogres on their way to the field of play with a badly sewn up bag might leave a trail of soot through the town.

"But things rubbed along pretty well on the whole – pretty well that is, until a certain Johannis Ogre was hurrying through our capital, Noddevilia, in the early hours of a dark winter's morning with a large bag of soot in each hand, intent on getting to a Soot Hurling Festival many kilometres away and somewhat distracted by the fact that he was very late. Now an ogre in a hurry is a fearsome thing, and at one point in the gloomy half light he came up against a Noddian boy. Luckily he just managed to avoid treading the boy underfoot, but Johannis was unusually tall even for an ogre – his hands came to nearly a half metre above the boy's head, which in turn put the soot bags just on a level with the unfortunate child's face, and so although Johannis himself missed the boy ... wallop!"

Here the Bailiff flailed her arms around her head in imitation of someone being struck full in the face by a large bag of soot.

"This brought matters to a head, so to speak. It took the poor child well over a week to wash himself completely clean, but the outcry lasted even longer. Johannis apologised – he even paid for new clothes and all the soap the boy could use – but the monarchs were forced to act, and this law was passed.

"The Noddians, of course, thought it sensible, but because soot hurling playing fields were, of necessity, many kilometres outside towns and villages, and because the festivals were liable to start at dawn and go on till dusk, this law put a serious obstacle in the way of many ogres who wished to pursue the sport. At the request of the oldest and most respected ogres, the law was altered to allow the carrying of bags on Midsummer's Night, as that was the night before the great Annual Soot Hurling competition, or ASH, as it was known, but most ogres quite reasonably complained that they needed the smaller games during the rest of the year to practise. Both monarchs refused to make any further changes – they dared not, as the Noddians would not have stood for it – so our ogres migrated, every single one of them, to the island of Fuliginea."

"Humph!" said Clotilde. She would have liked to have added all sorts of things to this "humph" but there was not time. Worst of all, there was not time to make any new laws to stop the ogres moving in, because it took many months to pass a law in Nodd.

"There doesn't seem to be much we can do, then," said the king, gloomily.

"Do you mind if I ask what it is you would like to do?" asked the Bailiff.

"A family of ogres is going to move next door to us," said the queen, "this very afternoon, and we've got to stop them."

"And why is that?" continued the Bailiff, with a puzzled tone to her voice.

The king and queen looked at the Bailiff in astonishment. Clovis glanced behind his chair furtively, and then said, very quietly.

"They eat children, Bailiff, they eat children. It's a well known fact."

Now the Bailiff may have been a bit lacking when it came to eyes, but she saw a lot further than most people nonetheless. She saw here, for instance, that the king, for all his royalty, was talking the most terrible nonsense. She also saw, though, that it would not be easy to convince him that it was nonsense.

"Well it's a fact that's escaped me," she replied, as she studied her toes. "There's no mention of any such thing in the tomes."

"But they left Nodd over a hundred years ago you said. They could have started after that," suggested the queen.

"Fuliginea is inhabited entirely by ogres," said the Bailiff. "If they eat children they must eat their own. Does that sound very likely?"

The queen and king looked a little taken aback at this. They shuffled about in their chairs for a moment or two and looked at the corners of the room.

"Well," said the queen, huffily, "everyone says they do, and everyone can't all be wrong."

"Yes, Bailiff – no stuff without whatsit, as they say," added Clovis.

"Humph," said the Bailiff, and got up. She could see that she would get no further that day. "I'd better be getting along. Thank you for the tea. I wish you good dreams."

And she fixed her single right eye firmly on the queen's right eye in a way that made the royal person feel most uncomfortable.

"Well I think that told her," said Clotilde, after the Bailiff had left the room. "She's getting a bit uppity, that Bailiff, in my opinion. Just because she knows a few old books off by heart she thinks she knows everything."

"Yes, my dear," replied Clovis, "she should get out of that tower of hers a bit more often and talk to ordinary folk."

"Yes – ordinary folk like us," said the queen.

But all this talk and worry and argument had worn her out, and she suddenly felt very, very tired.

"My dear," she said to Clovis, "I'm all in a tizz. I can't do any ruling when I'm in a tizz. I must have a nap. I think I'll just go into the garden and have forty winks before lunch, and we can talk more about this later."

And off she went.

*   *   *

The queen dozed in a comfortable chair in the shade, half listening to the children playing at the far end of the garden and half worrying about ogres.

"Got to do something … all very well that Bailiff treating it so lightly, they don't have children, just cats ... don't suppose ogres eat cats … not much of a meal in a cat for something that big …"

The sun was still not quite at its zenith, and the shade seemed to give no protection from its glaring, all-seeing eye. Even sound could not struggle through this heat and the noise of the children's laughter began to fade into a distant world somewhere far beyond the wilderness at the bottom of the palace garden.

"Could build a wall ..." thought Clotilde "... perhaps out of blackberries and hay ... nothing could get through that ... not even an Ogre in a hurry ... and umbrellas ... for the soot ... big boots ... better buy ..."

At this point a piercing scream tore through the air. The queen sat bolt upright.

"Ah – the children," she gasped, and ran down the garden in the blinding white heat of the day to where the scream had come from.

When she got to the wilderness she could see not a sign of them. She called their names, but the hot air seemed to stifle her voice and only the most feeble sound came out. In panic she ran from bush to bush, tree to tree, looking wildly about her.

Nothing.

But suddenly she noticed a huge gap in the hedge that ran between the gardens of the old palace and the new. The branches were torn and twisted, freshly broken. The meadow plants on either side of the hedge were trampled flat.

"Ah," cried Clotilde, "the ogres have arrived!"

And she ran towards the old palace through overgrown orchards and weed choked vegetable beds, following the frightful trail of crushed plants, forcing her way through the thick, clogged air that seemed, strangely, to get even hotter as she neared the tumble-down turrets of the long-deserted old palace.

But why had the air turned so grey? The queen looked up to the sky – it was not cloudy. Then she saw – every single chimney of the old palace was belching out thick, sooty smoke!

"Oh, the monsters! They're warming up the ovens!" cried out the terrified mother, as she flew across the lawn and up the steps to the terrace. Three quick paces and she threw herself against the great oak door.

It was bolted shut, of course, but Clotilde knew this building as well as her own palace – she had often played here as a child. She ran along the terrace to the left, down a short flight of narrow steps and around the corner. Here was the kitchen door, locked shut too, but that did not bother her in the least. Just beside this door was a wooden panel, about a metre square, which slid open to reveal a wooden box, cunningly made with various sized compartments. This box slid on a rail from the outside into the kitchen and was used many years ago by the gardeners to deliver their produce to the cook. It was now full of sea-shells and apple pips. Clotilde pulled out the box, pushed it off the rail, and there was her way in. She dropped on to all fours and scrambled through.

Immediately she felt a change. Inside it was damp and clammy – the brightness had fallen from the air and the dank smell of soot filled her nostrils. For a moment she paused for breath, and to listen. From some distant corner of the palace came a peculiar whirring noise, followed by a sharp, grating squeal that rang through the stone-clad corridors and was horrible to hear. In a flash the queen realised what it was – someone was sharpening knives on a circular grind-stone!

Out of the kitchen she flew, her whole mind intent on that terrible noise, but once she left the kitchen she became confused. It had all changed. Where was the staircase that led to the main floor? There was only a single passageway, and that seemed to go on for ever – it stretched out into the distance as far as the eye could see. The harsh grating sound filled it, and made the very flagstones quake. The queen had no choice: down the corridor she ran, hoping against hope that she might find a way out of it, but as she ran, the corridor got narrower and narrower, until she could hardly squeeze herself between the walls.

Desperate and terrified, Clotilde twisted herself round to try to go back, but she was stuck firm. She realised that the terrible sound had stopped, and all was now an eerie silence. Then, trembling down through the narrow space came a shrill child's voice: "Mummy! Mummy! Mummy!" Clotilde recognised it immediately – it was Bruin, and at the same time, the walls shook violently, as though the whole building had been grasped by a gigantic hand.

With a start, the queen woke up.

*   *   *

There are few things worse than being woken up suddenly. Your mind is all in bits and you feel as though your body is as well. It takes a few seconds to gather all the scattered fragments together and make you yourself again. Soon, however, Clotilde realised she was lying in her comfy garden chair, and that Bruin was shaking her by the shoulder with one hand and holding a small loaf of bread in the other, saying excitedly, "Mummy! Mummy! Mummy! It's true. They do eat children, the ogres – they do!"

Clotilde jumped up off her chair and clutched her child to her. "Oh, Bruin! Thank goodness you're safe. But where are they – where are those ogres?"

"They're in the old palace, they've just …"

"And Karlo, where's Karlo?" Clotilde demanded, her alarm suddenly returning.

"He's there with them, he's …"

But the queen did not wait for the rest of the answer. "Oh, my child!" she cried, and rushed off, leaving her daughter waving the loaf in the air, and calling out after her, "But, mummy, the loaf – I wanted to show you the loaf!"

*　　*　　*

The great front doors of the old palace stood wide open for the removals men who were transferring boxes and pieces of very large furniture from the huge lorry parked in the drive. Clotilde ran straight through into the hall where she stopped and screamed out at the top of her voice: "Karlo! Karlo!"

As she looked wildly around, desperately wondering which part of the palace to run to first, she heard a voice behind her.

"Hello, can I help?"

The queen spun round. Standing in the doorway – and taking up a good deal of it – was an unusually tall, thick-set man. It was Mr Ogre himself.

"Where's my son? What have you done with him?" she cried.

The man looked a little puzzled, but then smiled as he walked towards her. "Ah, you must be Karlo and Bruin's mother. I believe your son went back home. In fact, I think they both went, about five minutes ago."

The queen stared at the smiling face. It quite confused her – it was so open and pleasant. Could she be wrong about this? But suddenly all her fear welled up inside her again. No, he was lying. He had eaten her son and was just saying this to get rid of her so that he could go somewhere quiet and digest him. Oh, the beast!

She was about to hurl herself upon the monster when she heard a woman's voice calling down the stairs, "Jorvik, are you there?"

"Yes, dear," replied the Ogre.

"I can't find those childs anywhere," said the voice. "You haven't eaten them all, have you?"

The Ogre grinned broadly at Clotilde and winked in a conspiratorial manner, then looked up to where the voice was coming from. "Only one, Inger – it's been a long morning, you know!"

Clotilde gasped, staggered backwards, bumped into a packing case in the middle of the hall and sat down on it heavily. She felt giddy and sick and went very pale. The Ogre's smile disappeared and he stepped towards her.

"Inger, quickly, come down," he called out, and then, when he saw Bruin and Karlo coming through the door, "Ah, children, come here – your mother doesn't seem well."

Clotilde was dimly aware of feet clattering towards her from all directions at once on the bare stone floor. Then she heard, as though down the tunnel of a departing dream, her son's voice. "What's up, mum? Are you okay? We've been looking for you everywhere."

The wave of nausea passed as fast as it had come and she looked up. There, to her inexpressible joy, were her two children. She reached out and pulled them to her, tears of relief streaming down her face.

When she opened her eyes she saw the two ogres – two very large, good-natured and pleasant looking people regarding her with concern. All of a sudden, the queen realised what a fool she had been, and how rude she must seem to her new neighbours. A hot wave of shame flowed over her.

"Please … excuse me," she said, blushing deeply. "I don't know what came over me. You must be Mr and Mrs Ogre." She tried to stand up but Inger Ogre took her arm and sat her back down again .

"Think nothing of it," said Mrs Ogre. "You just sit there and get your breath back."

Bruin sat beside her on the packing case. "Look, mummy, look what Mr and Mrs Ogre gave us." And she handed her mother the small loaf she had tried to show her earlier.

Clotilde took the loaf. It was flat, about a hand's breadth across, and oval shaped. One side was a shiny golden colour, and was curiously moulded into the shape of a child.

"Their lorry got stuck in the drive," continued Bruin. "Its wheels just went round and round," giggled Karlo, "whirrrrr … "

"So Karlo and daddy and I went and helped, and they gave us these," said Bruin. "They're for luck."

"We call them 'childs'," said Mr Ogre. "When we move house, we give them to our new neighbours. I suppose it says that we are new in this place, like children. It's a very old custom."

"It's a very charming custom," said Clotilde, staring at the loaf. She was still feeling a bit hot and bothered, but luckily was distracted by the sight of her husband, half-running breathlessly into the hall.

"Clotilde!" he called. "Clotilde, my dear!"

23

Clovis shot a nervous smile at the new-comers as he came in and, waving his left hand vaguely in Clotilde's direction, stammered, "My ... my wife you know ... er ... queen ... " Then, stepping between her and the ogres, he seized her hand with his vagrant left paw and began winking and grimacing at her in the most peculiar way.

"Oaugh!" he mouthed, throwing his eyes back in his head, "Oaugh!" And he finished by putting a finger over his lips and winking in a very exaggerated way.

Clotilde hardly had time to wonder what this pantomime meant before the king switched his expression into a beaming smile, swung round, and said, "May I introduce you to my wife Clotilde, the queen – my dear, our new neighbours, Mr and Mrs Ogre."

"Yes, Clovis," said the queen, weakly, "we've sort of done that bit."

The king looked quickly back at Clotilde.

"Ah! Oh, well! No need to p ... p … pa ... pan ... pani ... panic!"

"No, Clovis, we've done that, too."

"Quite so, my dear," said the king, looking a little puzzled. Then, turning back to their guests, and putting his smile back on as he did so, he added, "Tell you what – it's lunch-time now and you must be a bit peckish what with all this bother. Won't you come with us and have a bite to eat, bit of a break, eh?"

Mr and Mrs Ogre happily agreed. Karlo jumped up, shouting, "Oh goody, we're having the Ogres for lunch!" And grabbing Mrs Ogre by the hand he dragged her towards the door whilst Clotilde, holding her daughter's hand, did her best to catch up.

"Hope there's something good," said the king in a confidential voice to Mr Ogre, as they followed along behind. "Didn't get much of a breakfast this morning, you know."

"Not to worry," said Mr Ogre, with a glint in his eye, "if there's nothing else we can always have one of the children." And he broke into loud guffaws of helpless laughter that made the empty hallway of the old palace ring with life.

Trouble with the Chickens

King Clovis scraped the knife roughly across his piece of toast as he tried to spread it with butter. He scraped so hard that crumbs flew off like sparks from a grindstone. The queen watched with dismay as they formed a brown layer on the clean white table cloth around his plate, but she knew it was no use saying anything. She knew that the king was in a bad mood.

At last the toast could take no more. There was not a piece of toast that ever came out of a toaster that could withstand the treatment being given to this poor, charred relative of the bread family. It shattered into a hundred tiny bits and flew all over the table. Bruin and Karlo ducked, partly to escape being hit by flying toast but partly also to hide their laughter. They, too, knew that their father was in a bad mood.

"Oh, drat and bother and great mouldy cornflakes!" cried Clovis in exasperation. "How on earth can a body be expected to make a decent breakfast out of these dried up old crusts!"

Clotilde was worried. It was king Clovis's day to rule, and she knew the effect that a bad breakfast would have on him.

"My dear," she said, in the most reasonable voice she could manage under the circumstances, "there's fruit juice, grapefruit, cereal and porridge. You could have bacon, sausages, baked beans and fried bread. You could have kippers if you wish, or rollmops or kedgeree; ham, cheese, hot buttered rolls, muffins, any number of various pastries and breads and I'm sure Chef Aygradouce could even rustle up devilled kidneys, not to mention ..."

"Yes, yes, my dear, but I want a boiled egg," sulked the king, his moustache drooping. "What's breakfast without boiled eggs."

"But you know it's only a temporary problem," replied the queen.

"Temporary! Temporary!" spluttered Clovis. "It's been a week since I last had a boiled egg for breakfast. Another week like this might make me lose my temper, you know."

"Some might say that had already happened," observed his wife to the cat that sat on the chair beside her. The cat sighed and buried her nose further under her tail.

"I'll tell you what," said the king to no one in particular (which is just as well since no one in particular was listening), "I'll go and sort those chickens out myself if Ancient Ovaparit can't do it by tomorrow. I'll teach them to go on strike."

"What does 'go on strike' mean, mummy?" asked Bruin.

"It means to stop working because you feel you're not being paid enough, or because you are upset about something," her mother replied.

"What are the chickens upset about?" came the next question.

"I don't know – and it's not much use asking your father," said the queen, seeing that her daughter was about to do just that, "because he doesn't know either. In fact, he doesn't even really know they are on strike."

"Well I don't know what else they're up to," said the king. "All they're doing is sitting on their perches like so many stuffed tea cosies and creaking – rweuuuurk-crhk-crhk-crhk-crhk – that's all they say, as if they haven't been oiled for a year."

"Perhaps that's what they need – a spot of oil," put in Karlo helpfully.

"I'll give them oil," muttered Clovis, "and I know where ..."

"Clovis!" said Clotilde, sharply. "Remember the children are present."

"Yes, yes – sorry, my dear! But it quite puts a body out of all patience not to get its egg every morning – and to think of those stupid birds just sitting there, creaking – rweuuuurk-crhk-crhk-crhk-crhk!"

"Well, you'd better go and see Ancient Ovaparit as soon as possible – he might have found the answer by now."

The king sighed deeply. "Indeed he might – one can but hope. But first I must see Bailiff Left. I emailed her yesterday and asked her to put her mind to this chicken business and she'll be here very shortly."

"Well, if anyone can find out what's wrong with those chickens, it'll be the Bailiffs," said his wife, trying her best to sound encouraging.

"That's true, my dear," replied Clovis. He smiled weakly at her and then turned his gaze back to the breakfast table which he surveyed gloomily. "Well, there's not much point in sitting here any more. Better get ready for the Bailiff."

The king rose and stalked morosely from the room, his moustache flopping listlessly as he went.

* * *

At that same moment, Ancient Ovaparit was sitting, as he did every morning after his breakfast, inside the royal chicken-run. He was having his daily gossip with his chickiebirdies, as he called them. Like king Clovis, he was the picture of gloom. Luckily for the king, though, that was as far as the resemblance went since Ancient Ovaparit looked like no other creature in Nodd – except, that is, for the chickens that sat around him.

It was not so much his feet – though they were very large and flat, with long thin toes that spread out like a chicken's claw. Nor was it his two thin little legs, like the stubs of a couple of well-used pencils, which supported his squat, round body. It was mainly, it has to be said, his face which gave the game away. He had no chin, and purple-veined, drooping cheeks hung down below a mouth almost hidden by the huge beak of a nose. Set deeply back on either side of the nose were two tiny, round, watery eyes, the pupils of which never seemed to move. But above all it was his hair which set the seal on his chickenhood. This hair was his crowning glory: sandy-red in colour, it grew straight up and fell backwards at the top in a series of waves, for all the world like the comb on a cockerel's head.

Ancient Ovaparit was peculiarly proud of this hair, and he would spend ages every morning in front of his bathroom mirror combing it upwards in great sweeping movements until he had got the top edge falling in a series of perfect, soft, undulations, which became gradually smaller from the front to the back of his head.

Why he did this nobody knew. To begin with, nine days out of ten the only other living creatures to see him were his chickens. But also, and perhaps more to the point, all his trouble was wasted the moment he began to move because, when Ancient Ovaparit walked, his head jerked violently back and forth and in a matter of seconds his carefully combed coiffure – or carefully coiffured comb – was flopping about all over the place. But then, as Bailiff Left had so rightly observed, we all have our little foibles, and why should poor Ovaparit not be allowed his.

To complete this portrait, though, we ought to note that, since the Ancient's head jutted out somewhat ahead of his body when he walked, it was necessary for him to maintain his balance by sticking his bottom out in the opposite direction. Here it supported his coarse brown tweed jacket which stuck up behind him like a tail in final mockery of the birds it was his job in life to look after.

Chickens, no doubt, are very pleased to look the way they do – after all, they look like what they are. However, to be a human being and look like a chicken must be counted a misfortune, and other human beings being what they are, that misfortune would frequently and forcibly be brought to the attention of the person who suffered it. For that reason, had you seen him on any other day, sitting inside the royal chicken yard, Ancient Ovaparit would have looked miserable. On this particular morning, though, his mind was troubled with the same gloomy thoughts as were causing king Clovis so much anguish which was the refusal of the chickens to lay, and it was on that topic that he was trying to engage his birds in conversation.

"Come now, my dearies," he crooned. "What be getting you so down in the beaks?"

"Rweuuuurk-crhk-crhk," said Henry the cockerel, miserably, by which he meant, "What's the point?"

"Well I know you'm sad, my birdies," responded the Ancient, who fancied that he understood every word the chickens said (quite mistakenly, of course, since Chicken is far too difficult for any human being to learn). "But why'm you so sad?"

"Rweuuuurk-crhk-crhk," said Henry, meaning this time, "We're all going to die." And now you can probably see the problem with Chicken: there is only one word in the language and it can mean whatever the speaker wants it to.

"But the days be getting warmer all the time," argued Ancient Ovaparit.

"Rweuuuurk-crhk-crhk (what a stupid old git this man is)," replied Henry.

"Ah well, you'm right there," said the Ancient. "'Twas a sharp frost this morning, but that b'aint nothing to a well-feathered bird like you."

"Rweuuuurk-crhk-crhk (but at least we won't have to put up with him much longer)," muttered Henry, darkly.

Ancient Ovaparit scratched his head. This last comment had him puzzled. "All right then, my chickiebirdies," he said at last. "I'sl think on what I can do." And much to Henry's relief he fell silent and became engrossed in his own thoughts.

It was at this point that Karlo arrived, determined to see if he could find out what had upset the chickens and whether, by oil or any other means, he could make them better.

"Hello!" said Karlo to the birds as he looked at them over the fence. "What's up with you, then?"

"Ah, you may well axe, young'un. My poor liddle chickiebirdies!" came a voice from amongst the chickens .

Karlo almost jumped out of his skin. "Oh! Ancient Ovaparit – I didn't notice you there," he exclaimed.

"No, people seldom does," complained the old man. "But why I dussn't know, as I always be here. But what d'bring you down these parts?"

"Father said the chickens are on strike and that they're creaking."

"Ah, they may be on strike aright, but I dussn't know as they'm creaking."

"I wondered if they might need oiling. I've heard of a special oil for cods' livers, so I thought there might be one for chickens' beaks. What do you think?"

Ancient Ovaparit chuckled. "Rweuuuurk-crhk-crhk-crhk-crhk. I d'think you got that a bit wrong, young Karlo. Cod's Liver Oil b'aint summat you d'put into a cod's liver – it be summat you d'take out of a cod's liver. It be ..."

He stopped. His mouth hung open and his watery, pale eyes stared into space. Then he blinked a few times and turned back to Karlo.

"Aye – it be full of them vitalthings ... flap me! I did never think o' that ..." Whereupon he almost flew out of the yard, head jerking to and fro, and disappeared into his cottage, a tumble-down wooden shack that many visitors mistook for the chicken house.

Karlo, being used to the strange ways of the Ancient, took little notice, but continued looking at the chickens.

"They certainly do look upset," he thought. "Perhaps they just need cheering up. I know – Bruin and I can put on a show for them. I bet they'd like that."

He stood for a while, going over in his mind the various entertainments that he and his sister could lay on for them: some scenes from a pantomime, Punch and Judy, a song and dance routine, a few magic tricks, or a magic lantern show, perhaps. Whatever they did, though, there was one thing he was quite sure of – they had to do it straight away, as their father's temper was getting worse by the hour and if he did not get his eggs for breakfast again soon, not only the family but the whole island could suffer.

As Karlo set off back home, Henry turned to Mary, his fifteenth wife, and muttered, "Rweuuuurk-crhk-crhk (these humans are so stupid). Rweuuuurk-crhk-crhk-crhk-crhk (they obviously haven't realised that the sky is going to fall down tomorrow)."

For that, no less, was what had been predicted the week before in The Daily Eggspress by that famous feathered soothsayer, Chicken Licken. It was by no means the first time that Chicken Licken had made this prophecy (and it probably would not be the last) but this time the royal birds were convinced by it – for no particular reason, as chickens did not think according to reason – and they had decided that if the end of the world was coming, there was absolutely no point in working any more.

*   *   *

King Clovis showed Bailiff Left into the living room and handed her a cup of tea.

"Now then, Bailiff," he said, "What about my chickens. The pesky birds have simply stopped laying – gone on strike it would appear. Have you got any ideas about why that might be?"

"I most certainly have, king Clovis," said Bailiff Left. "I dreamed about them last night."

King Clovis was agog. "Did you really?" he said. "Tell on, Bailiff Left, tell on."

"Well," she started, "I was standing on a jetty looking out to sea, when I noticed a small boat tied up just below where I was standing. In it was a man dressed as a clown. I called out to him, 'hello, have you just arrived?' He gave me a very blank look in return, so I raised my voice a little and asked, 'do you speak Noddian?' He gave me another look, even more blank that the last if that was possible, which I took to mean, 'no!' But then he suddenly shouted, 'I have a terrible headache, but I've been in the jungle so I couldn't get any tablets.' Of course, this being a dream, I understood his language perfectly and even spoke it, so 'why is that?' I enquired. 'Because,' he replied, 'the-parrots-eat-'em-all.'

"I next asked him how he had got to Nodd and he replied, 'rowed.' So I then asked, 'and what are you going to do now?' 'I land,' he announced, getting out of his boat. I reckoned it must have been a long journey so I asked him how he had amused himself whilst at sea. Pointing to a pile of old newspapers and magazines in the bottom of his boat he replied, 'Read.'

"I looked around at that point, and saw that we were no longer on the jetty but on a grassy bank full of rabbit holes. He waved his arm and said, 'warren'.

"'Yes,' I said. 'We're plagued by rabbits on our island, and we could do with a few more weasels and stoats – though I could never tell the difference between them'.

"'Ah,' said the clown, 'I can help you there – a weasel's weasily recognised and a stoat's s'totally different.'

"At this point he laughed so much that his head fell off, and I saw that he actually was a weasel – or perhaps he was a stoat –– I'm afraid his method of telling the difference wasn't really very helpful after all."

Bailiff Left stopped and looked at the king.

"Er ... yes ...?" said Clovis.

"Well, that's it, king," said the Bailiff.

"I must have missed something, Bailiff," said the king, still puzzled. "I ... er ... thought you said you had a dream about chickens."

"Yes – don't you see. First was his silly joke about the headache tablets – 'the parrots eat 'em all'."

Now it was the king's turn to look blank. "Paracetamol, you see ..." said the Bailiff.

"Yes, yes, Bailiff – I get the joke, for what it's worth," said Clovis, rather irritably. "What I don't get is what it's got to do with chickens."

"Ah, that's the next bit. To begin with he was letting me know that everything he said was a pun. Do you remember what he said in answer to my three questions? 'Rowed', 'I land', and 'read' – Rhode Island Red, you see. That's the name of a breed of chicken, isn't it?"

"Oh! Now I get it," exclaimed the king, suddenly perking up. "And then 'warren' – not really rabbit warren at all but the Warren, another breed of chicken. And that's what I've got, Bailiff, Warrens – good layers ..." for a moment the excitement went out of his voice and his moustache drooped, "... humph, well, ought to be good layers. But what about this stoat and weasel business, Bailiff – I don't understand that at all."

"Well, he was one himself, of course, and he was getting breeds of chickens all confused with other things. I'd hazard a guess, king, that what's going on in your chicken-run is that the birds are being confused somehow or other by weasels – or stoats -– or both – and that's putting them off their laying."

"Great cornflakes, Bailiff!" cried the king, leaping out of his chair, "I believe you've got it! I must go and tell Clotilde."

Just before he got to the door, though, he turned and ran back. "But hang on a minute – did this weasel chap tell you how to deal with them?"

"No, I slipped into another dream after that," said Bailiff Left. "Very silly it was too – a bus was going along a road and bumping into everything – trees, walls, hedges, bus-stops. Whatever it went near it blundered into."

"Ha!" cried Clovis. "That's it! A blunder-bus! My old great-grandfather's blunderbuss! A dose of that will sort 'em out all right! Ah, thank you Bailiff, thank you – I think you've solved the problem."

The king was heading for the door again when he remembered his manners.

"Ah! Sorry, Bailiff – you'll stay for a spot of lunch, won't you?"

"Why, thank you, king, I don't mind if I do," replied Bailiff Left, much relieved that she was not going to be left to walk home on an empty stomach.

"Won't be soufflé, of course, or omelette," said Clovis apologetically as he led the way to the dining room, "but I'm sure we'll manage something, and after lunch I'll get out that old blunderbuss and give it a good clean and oiling, and then tonight – aha! – I'll be waiting for those little beggars down by the chicken houses. One good dose from the barrel of that old elephant blaster will blow them at the moon – oh, most sweet! Ah, Bailiff, you've no idea what a weight you've lifted from my mind. I can't thank you enough. Must tell Clotilde your dream – parrots eat 'em all! Hahaha! Most amusing when you think about it. Yes, very droll!"

*   *   *

Later, as dusk began to draw its curtains on the day, Karlo and Bruin made their way down to the chicken-run, carrying between them a huge cardboard box which contained all they needed to put on a first-rate magic lantern slide show. They had decided on this as the most suitable entertainment for their audience of chickens for several reasons: first, their collection of slides consisted mostly of pictures of people dressed up to look like various kinds of birds and they thought that chickens would find this particularly funny; second, it did not involve learning any lines, which they had no time to do; and third, it could be seen in the dark – Punch and Judy might be very amusing, but only if you could see what was going on. Best of all, though, their magic lantern was an antique thing that used a candle to produce the light rather than electricity, so they could work it just as well in the middle of the woods as anywhere else.

When they got to the chicken-run all the birds were in their huts. Ancient Ovaparit had obviously shut them up early for some reason, but this suited the children very well.

"Couldn't be better," whispered Karlo. "As long as we don't make any noise setting things up it will be a complete surprise for the chickens when we let them out, so, no more talking now – okay?"

Bruin gave a thumbs up to show that she understood and agreed.

Working quickly together (they had planned everything thoroughly in advance) they hung up one of their bedsheets between two trees to form the screen. By the time they had done this the remaining daylight had gone. A half moon provided a little light in the open space of the chicken-run, but Karlo and Bruin had to set up the lantern under the trees outside the fence at the other end of the enclosure, where they worked quietly mainly by touch and feel.

Whilst they were busy, another nocturnal visitor crept stealthily down the path and into the trees at the end of the chicken-run where the two children were working, and it was as well that it was too dark to see amongst those trees, and that they were too engrossed in what they were doing to hear the slight sounds made by the newcomer as he moved, because this was not the sort of thing the average child wanted to meet in the woods in the middle of the night with only a few dozen chickens to turn to for help.

The body of this ghastly creature was draped in a heavy, black cloak that reached from the shoulders to the ground. His feet, wrapped up in towels tied all round with thick garden twine, stuck out below the cloak. No face was visible. If there was one, it was concealed behind the fronds of a large bush which seemed to take the place of the creature's head. Obviously this person wished to move silently and blend into the landscape, though actually the overall effect was more like a mobile scarecrow.

As he padded softly between the trees he slipped out from under his cloak a large, shiny, trumpet shaped object. He then lay down in a position from which he had a good view of the chicken houses and the moon-lit run, put the object to his shoulder, pointed it through the fence, and settled in for what he clearly thought was going to be a long wait.

Once he was comfortable and lying quite still, king Clovis – for this extraordinary figure was none other than he – became aware of a very slight noise coming from behind the trees a few metres to his left.

"Aha!" he thought. "That'll be those pesky weasels – or stoats – preparing their mischief for the evening. I wonder what they've got planned for my poor chickens tonight."

He strained his ears to see if he could gather any clues from the noise.

"Sounds like glass tinkling," he thought, "and metal rubbing against metal? Bottles and cans, perhaps ... ?"

A sudden and terrible thought sprang to his mind.

"My kneecaps! That's it! The devils – they're getting the birds drunk every night! No wonder

they can't do anything but sit there and creak –
they've got beastly hang-overs every morning!
Well, my furry friends, I've got something here
that'll make your party go with a bang tonight!"

As he lay in wait his mind began to form
pictures of the stoats (or weasels) setting up a bar
amongst the trees, decking it out with all the gaudy
glitter that might tempt those bird-brained chickens
to gambol down the primrose path to an alcoholic
hell. The images became more and more vivid.
Soon the king's head, bowed down by the cares of
the day (not to mention the weight of the bush on
top of it) began to sink, so that he failed to notice a
shadowy figure quietly open the gate into the
chicken-run and drag itself across the enclosure
with a ponderous, jerking shuffle – a doomed
monstrosity from the bottomless pit it appeared to
be, hauling along the ball and chain that should
have kept it in the dreadful dungeon from which it
had escaped.

But Ancient Ovaparit moved slowly because
he was weighed down by two heavy buckets, each
one containing several litres of the best quality
Cod's Liver Oil that Nodd could provide. That
chance remark by Karlo in the morning had
reminded him that this oil was a splendid source of
vitamins A and D, both vital to the well being of
chickens and highly beneficial to their laying. His

tasks for the day completed, he had shut up the birds for the night, sidled into town, and bought up the island's entire stock of Grade A1 Cod's Liver Oil. Now he was determined that his chickiebirdies should wait no longer for their treat.

On reaching the rear door of the first of the chicken houses, he put down his buckets and knelt on the ground to open it. As the handles of the metal buckets dropped a loud clang rang out across the clearing.

King Clovis instantly started out of his snooze and stared at where the noise had come from. He could see nothing because Ancient Ovaparit was on the other side of the chicken house from him and, because it was about a metre high, the Ancient was completely hidden by it. However, convinced that the weasels (or stoats) were up to something, the king raised himself slowly and carefully into a sitting position and brought the blunderbuss up to his shoulder.

Bruin and Karlo, who had been too busy with fitting up their magic lantern to notice the arrival of Ancient Ovaparit, also heard the clang of the bucket handles. They, too, jumped, and looked at each other in momentary fear.

But they had no time to waste. Karlo put his finger to his lips and gestured that the lantern was all ready. Carefully, he picked up a box of matches and took one out.

Ancient Ovaparit fumbled with the catch to the door of chicken house. It seemed to be stuck, so he put one hand on the roof to steady himself. As he did this he raised up his head so that it was almost level with his hand.

"Drat this dangblasted rusty old thing," muttered the Ancient as he pulled and fiddled at the catch.

By the feeble light of the half-moon Clovis could now just make out two small, sinuous shapes on the roof of the chicken house. One seemed to be hanging over the edge of the roof, the other was dancing and prancing about, waving and weaving, bobbing up and down. He strained his ears to try and hear what they were saying to one another.

Then first shape disappeared: it must have jumped into the hut. The king dared wait no longer. He pulled gently on the trigger of his blunderbuss and the stilly darkness of the night suddenly erupted in thunder and fire, and for a split second it seemed as though the world was one huge, roaring flame.

Ancient Ovaparit felt a red-hot tempest tear across the top of his head, taking with it his fine comb of hair. Leaping to his feet, he knocked over the two buckets, tried to run, slipped, and found

himself face down in a huge, rapidly spreading
puddle of evil fishy-smelling oil. Scrabbling
desperately onto his hands and knees he looked
wildly around and saw, in the air above him at the
end of the run, a sight that struck him rigid with
fear.

As chance would have it, at the very second
the king's blunderbuss had gone off, Karlo had put
his match to the candle of the magic lantern, so a
powerful beam of light now shone out across the
clearing to reveal the sheet that the children had
rigged up as their screen. Ripped from its
fastenings by the explosion from the gun, it now
seemed to be floating in mid-air, though in fact it
was simply draped over a sapling, and waving
gently in the after-shock of the blast.

"Angels defend us!" cried the poor old
Ancient. "It be the ghost of my old feyther come
from the grave to chide his wicked son!"

A voice boomed out from behind him. "Great
Cornflakes! Is that you Ancient Ovaparit?"

The Ancient swung round towards the voice
but found himself dazzled by what looked like a
single, cold eye staring angrily at him from the
other side of the clearing. At the same time he
became aware that the chicken house he was
holding on to was vibrating violently. He was in no
fit state of mind to realise that this was caused by

fear-crazed chickens flapping around inside like lemmings in a sack. Ancient Ovaparit put it down to the mysterious powers of that shimmering white eye.

"Oh mercy! It be aliens!" he shrieked. "Feyther, feyther, they'm come to abstract me!"

Making one last desperate effort he got to his feet and tried to run, only to find himself slithering, totally out of control, across the slick of fishy oil towards the spectral figure of his father waiting for him amongst the trees.

"Rweuuuuurrrrk-crhk-crhk-crhk-crhk-crhk-crhk-crhk-RWEUURRRKKK!" he cried, as he hit the fence and toppled over it into the bramble bushes. There he lay on his back, squeaking and gibbering at the ghostly sheet above him, until Clovis, Karlo and Bruin ran to his assistance.

*   *   *

It took the king and his two children a good quarter of an hour to calm the Ancient down. Once he was finally persuaded, though, that there were neither ghosts nor aliens on the loose in his chicken-run he staggered to his feet.

"I mun see that my p-p-poor chickiebirdies b-be a'right," he stammered, as he walked shakily over to the huts. "They be gone mortal quiet all on a sudden."

The others followed. There was certainly a worrying silence on the part of the chickiebirdies.

But as he peered anxiously over Ancient Ovaparit's shoulder into the first of the huts the king's heart leapt, and he let out a whoop of delight. There amongst the straw he could just pick out the glimmer of several freshly laid eggs!

"They've been laying – it worked – it worked!" cried Clovis. He grabbed hold of the Ancient and swung him round in a clumsy dance which ended with both of them sitting in the puddle of Cod's Liver Oil.

As they sat there, breathless but happy, Henry stalked nervously out of the hut followed by several of his wives, one of whom said in a quavering voice to her friend, "Rweuuuurk-crhk-crhk-crhk-crhk (well, my dear, that dreadful noise just frightened the eggs out of me)."

"What's she saying, Ancient, what's she saying?" asked king Clovis eagerly.

"She be saying, king," replied Ancient Ovaparit, "unless I be mightily mistaken, that they'm all very sorry birds for causing this here kerfuffle." Henry and some of his wives flapped up onto the roof, and looked dolefully at the white eye of the magic lantern.

"Rweuuuurk-crhk-crhk-crhk (what's that bright light lying in the trees over there)?" asked Emily, wife number twenty-three.

"Rweuuuurk-crhk-crhk (it's only the moon, my dear)," replied Henry.

"They've done seen the light at last," translated the Ancient.

"Rweuuuurk-crhk-crhk-crhk-crhk, rweuuuurk-crhk-crhk-creuuurhk! (if that's the moon, then Chicken Licken was right: the sky has indeed fallen down. It's the end of the world!)" cried Mary

"They do reckon everything be fine again, now," added Ancient Ovaparit.

Henry looked down sadly at the group of smiling humans behind him. "Rweuuuurk-crhk-crhk-crhk-crhk (yes, and that lot are so stupid they haven't even noticed yet)!"

Bruin and the Wolf

There was something special in the air that day, thought Bruin, as she and her brother Karlo strolled along Horngates Lane. It was not just the fresh green leaves, the drifts of white may blossom and the dusty hazel catkins in the hedgerows. It was not even the promise of those lazy summer days that were only a bat-squeak away. No – something utterly new and unknown was, she felt, being trumpeted by the daffodils that still crowded the banks of the path, something exciting and adventuresome, something which, she was sure, must be only just round the next bend in the lane.

The two children had set out to see the Bailiffs, partly to say hello, as they often did, and partly because there and back was about right for a morning walk in Spring. But this lane had plenty to offer in the way of entertainment, with the sea a hundred metres or so across the fields to the left, and Wyrd Woods about the same distance over the fields to the right, so if you came across something interesting, you could always change your mind and pursue that, and at any moment, thought

Bruin, that something interesting was about to happen.

Just then, her brother, who was standing on a stile leading into the fields by the woods, beckoned her over excitedly. "Bruin! Bruin! Come and look – look at the flowers in this field – they're moving!"

Bruin ran over. Was this true, or was her brother merely imagining things, as he so often did? But no, Karlo was quite right: the field was full of what looked like tiny white flowers which were slowly opening and closing their broad, flat petals all together!

"How peculiar! Let's see what they are," cried Bruin, jumping over the stile and running into the field. But as she did so, the flowers rose into the air, as though someone had lifted up and shaken a lace table cloth. It was then that Bruin realised what they were – a host of tiny, pure white butterflies.

For a moment, they seemed to hover over the grass, but as Bruin ran towards them they floated, like a magic carpet, towards the woods.

"Come on, Karlo, let's follow them," she called back to her brother.

"Hold on a moment, Bruin," Karlo shouted. "They're heading for the woods."

"So what?" came the reply.

But Wyrd Woods frightened Karlo. No matter how sunny the day, it was always dark amongst those trees, and you never heard birds singing in there.

"Well … er … they might not want you to follow them."

Bruin stopped and watched the shimmering carpet of butterflies. It, too, stopped about ten metres away.

"Yes they do – see, they're waiting for us."

And sure enough, as Bruin carried on towards them, the butterflies started to move too, at the same pace as her.

Karlo began to follow reluctantly. He watched as first the butterflies and then his sister disappeared as she squeezed through a narrow gap in the hedge that surrounded the woods.

"Bruin! Bruin!" he cried out. "Don't go into the woods – you'll get lost."

There was no reply.

"Or fall down a boggart hole!"

Still no reply.

"Or get frazzled by a dragon!"

Still silence.

Karlo was really worried now. He ran to the gap and peered in, but what he saw made him gasp with surprise. Bruin was running down a tunnel of shimmering white blossom towards the butterflies which swirled like huge flakes of snow ahead of her. It looked to Karlo as if his sister was running into a blizzard – as if for a moment, winter had strangely returned to the warm spring day.

"Look, Karlo!" called out Bruin as she ran. "They're like a big, fluffy snow-ball, floating along through the air!"

The sight of all that blossom made Karlo feel happier about going into the woods, so he set off after Bruin.

"Or a cloud of feathers without a pillow-case round it!" continued the girl.

"More like a lot of feathers that have forgotten they aren't attached to a bird any longer!" said Karlo as he caught up with his sister.

"I know what it reminds me of," cried Bruin, "I've been trying to think of it all this time – one of those glass domes full of water that you shake to make a snow-storm appear!"

"Well I wish it would settle on something, then," said Karlo, who was beginning to worry again at going so far into Wyrd Woods.

But they did not have to wait long for this to happen. Very soon they came out of the tunnel into a brightly lit glade. Here the butterflies stopped and danced high up in the shafts of sunlight that streamed through the roof of the wood. Below their softly billowing canopy sat the wolf.

For a few moments, children and animal looked at each other.

"What do you think it is, Bruin?" asked Karlo at last.

"I don't know, but it's beautiful – so soft and quiet looking," replied Bruin.

"I think it looks rather sad," said her brother.

"It must be lost," said Bruin. "That's why the butterflies have brought us here. It's lost and needs help. We'd better take it home – we can adopt it."

"But we haven't the faintest idea what it is. How will we know what to give it to eat if we don't know what it is?"

"It looks sort of like a dog. Are you a dog?" Bruin asked the strange animal.

The wolf shook her head. She lowered her slim, grey muzzle, opened her mouth as though about to yawn, then lifted her head towards the sky and howled a low, eerie howl that sounded as though it came from miles away.

"Uuoooowwwwwwww."

"Oh great! Is that its name?" said Karlo, "How on earth do you say that." He lifted up his head and tried to imitate the wolf. "Eh – oooooooo!"

It was not a very good imitation, but it seemed to please the wolf, because she got up and walked over to the two children with her nose pointing to the ground, her ears flat and the end of her tail wagging. When she reached them, she lay down and rolled over, paws pedalling in the air, as though asking to be petted. Bruin knelt beside her and stroked her tummy and the wolf stretched up her two front paws and put them around Bruin's neck in a gentle, almost loving embrace. But as she did so her left paw caught in Bruin's necklace, a beautiful piece of red Venetian glass in the shape of a heart on a delicate gold chain, and pulled it off. Bruin, however, noticed nothing, and carried on stroking her new friend.

"Well, that must be it, then," said Karlo as he knelt down beside his sister to stroke the animal. "It's an Eh-oo. Hello, Eh-oo." And the wolf let out a contented little sigh as the two children petted her.

"We can't call it that, though," protested Bruin. "We've got to give it a proper name."

She thought for a moment, looking at the wolf as she stroked it.

"I know – it looked sad when we first saw it, so we'll give it a name to make it happy. How about 'Joy'?" said Bruin.

The wolf made some throaty, grunting noises as she rubbed her back on the ground and smiled the smile of a wolf.

"See, it's much happier already,' said Bruin. "Pretty Joy! Sweet Joy I call you."

Suddenly Bruin jumped up. "I know what we can do – we'll take Joy to the Bailiffs. They'll tell us what sort of an animal she is."

"Okay," said Karlo, with a sigh. "But I don't think this is your most brilliant idea, Bruin."

He looked across the clearing to where the butterflies still fluttered in the dusty shafts of sunlight. "You're not going to adopt them, too, are you?"

"No," replied Bruin, as she watched the restless cloud slowly melting away into the trees around the glade. "I think they can look after themselves."

"That's a relief," said her brother. "I couldn't have thought up names for all of them."

*   *   *

Bailiff Left was pleased to see the twins and she threw the door wide open to welcome them in, but because she stood aside to their right as the little party entered she did not see Joy trotting along behind them – the wolf, of course, was on her blind side!

She led the way into the front room, where she and Bailiff Right had been having their lunch.

"Hello, Bailiff Right," said Bruin. "We've brought ..."

But at this point it seemed as though someone had managed to tread at the same time on all twelve tails of the cats who had been busy snoozing peacefully in various parts of the room. Letting out twelve screeches, each one of which could have torn a tea-towel in half, the terrified creatures leapt on to the nearest table, shelf, or mantelpiece, sending vases, cups, flowers, sandwiches, candles and candlesticks, books, plates, lamps, tea, ornaments, biscuits, bananas, picture frames, clocks, saucers, cakes, teapots, plants, apples, statues and statuettes and anything else moveable, breakable or spillable hurtling to the floor with a crash that made everyone jump – including the cats, who, having already just done that, looked as though they were on trampolines. When they finally stopped bouncing they sat, looking like porcupines with toilet brushes for tails, glaring down at Joy. Finally, all together, they let out a single, rasping, very angry sounding hiss.

"Ah!" said Bailiff Right, looking across the wreckage of the room and her lunch, "it's a wolf."

Once the mess had been cleared up, Joy put in the kitchen with some food and a bowl of water, and the cats stroked sufficiently to restore them to their usual state of calm, the humans were able to sit down.

"I'm really sorry, Bailiffs," said Bruin. "We just had no idea. "

"Don't worry, Bruin, no great damage done – nothing valuable was broken, and you weren't to know," said Bailiff Left, as she brought in a tray with a fresh supply of sandwiches and drinks. "But where on earth did you come across this wolf?"

Bruin told the story of how they had found Joy, and explained that they had decided to adopt her.

"You decided," Karlo corrected her. "I told you I thought it was a mad idea. I don't suppose our cats will like Joy any more than the Bailiffs' did."

"The cats," said Bailiff Right, "are the least of your problems. What about your parents? I doubt if they're going to welcome a wolf with open arms!"

"But they're very fond of animals," said Bruin. "I'm sure they won't mind."

"The trouble is," said Bailiff Left, who had been looking carefully at her toes whilst Bruin told her story, "it's not really up to them. You see, the sheep farmers of Nodd simply would not allow a wolf on the island. They'll tell you that there's nothing a wolf likes to eat more than a tender, juicy little lamb and since these animals don't live here naturally, they would say it was madness to allow one in."

"It's only one wolf," said Bruin.

"Try telling that to a sheep farmer. They would say that one wolf can eat a lot of lambs in its lifetime, Just imagine, if it ate three a week and lived to be fifteen years old – which is the average age for a wolf – let me see ... " Bailiff Left did some sums in her head.

"Better add an extra one for Yursend," put in Bailiff Right, thinking of the Noddian new year holiday which was celebrated with an exceptionally huge meal.

"And an extra one for its birthday, too, I suppose," said Karlo. His sister shot him an angry glance.

"Yes, well, that comes to two thousand, three hundred and seventy lambs altogether," said Bailiff Right. "That's a lot of lambs."

"Oh dear," said Bruin, "I see what you mean. But she's so sweet. I'm sure she could be taught not to eat lambs."

"I can't imagine our farmers giving her the chance to learn. They'll all know the story of Tenant Snurdle," said Bailiff Left.

" Tenant Snurdle!" Karlo exclaimed. "Who was he?"

"He was an extremely quarrelsome old farmer. He got the notion into his head that the best police were ex-criminals, and the best game-keepers were ex-poachers, so he brought two wolves over to Nodd with the intention of training them to protect his flocks from other wolves. When it was pointed out that there weren't any wolves in Nodd to protect his flocks from, he replied that there were now, because he had two, so all the more reason to get them on our side and train them to look after sheep."

Bruin could see that Tenant Snurdle was going to be a stumbling block to her plans. She hardly dared ask for the end of the story. "And ... ?"

"Well, he ended up with no sheep and two very fat wolves, of course," said the Bailiff.

"And then what happened to the wolves?" asked Bruin, worried that there might be a rather awful end to this story.

"Oh, they were taken back to where they came from. Nobody blamed them – they were just doing what came naturally to them. It was entirely Snurdle's fault. Mind you, despite that, all the other farmers gave him a sheep each from their flocks so that he could set up again, but only on the promise that he would never bring any other animals to the island of any sort whatsoever."

"And he kept his promise," added Right, "but he turned his energies instead to breeding a sheep whose fleece would fall off of its own accord – to save the trouble of shearing them, you see – and then he ended up with a flock of completely bald sheep."

"Ah, poor old Snurdle," said Left. "It wasn't just his sheep, either. His whole family went as bald as eggs, and he wasted what was left of his money trying to find a cure for it. Utterly hopeless, of course, but it never really bothered him. 'I came into this world bald and penniless,' he said, 'and I see no reason why I shouldn't leave it bald and penniless' – and so he did."

Bruin had long since lost interest in the troubles of Tenant Snurdle and wanted to get the Bailiffs back on to the problem of how she could keep her new pet.

"So isn't there anything we can do?" she asked.

The two Bailiffs exchanged a quick glance, left eye to right eye, and Left said, "Leave her with us tonight. We'll look after her, and you two go home and sleep on it. You might find something will come to you in a dream – there's nothing like dreaming for sorting things out, as you know. Don't say anything to your parents until tomorrow. In fact, perhaps best to wait until we've been able to talk to them. We'll come over later in the morning with the wolf."

The two children thanked the Bailiffs and Bruin went into the kitchen to say good-bye to Joy. When she put her arm round the wolf's neck, Joy nuzzled her, breathing her hot, damp breath into the girl's ear.

"I think," said Bailiff Right, "that wolf is trying to tell you something."

*   *   *

The butterflies came back in Bruin's dream. Fluttering silently around her they guided her through the wood to a clearing very like the one in which she and Karlo had found Joy. This time, however, it was a different wolf that she saw under the billowing canopy of confetti – a much bigger and older looking animal.

Bruin went and sat in front of him. She felt very small. The wolf seemed to tower over her, stretching up high into the roof of the forest. Way up in the distance she saw him looking back down at her along his slender, intelligent muzzle.

"Hello," he said. "I'm glad you could come."

"I'm very pleased to be here, and to meet you," replied Bruin politely.

"I must tell you about Joy," said the wolf, "how she came to be on Nodd, and why she needs looking after."

"Ah, yes, I'd like that very much," said Bruin.

"You see," continued the wolf, " when she was very young and still learning to hunt she broke a leg whilst chasing a sheep. She was taken in by two humans who helped the leg heal and after that, because of their kindness, she felt she could never hunt sheep again. Now, we don't eat sheep that much, you know – not anything like as much as humans say we do – for the simple reason that it's much more dangerous to hunt something that's watched and protected. But if there's no other food, well, then we have to, so it would have been very difficult for Joy to stay with us. I don't expect you to understand this – you're only a human after all – but we felt it would be better for her to go somewhere else, where wolves aren't so feared and persecuted, so we decided that she had best go and live with you in Nodd"

"I'm afraid she might have come to the wrong place," said Bruin. "I know we don't have any wolves in Nodd, but they're just as much disliked by our farmers."

"Don't worry," said the wolf, "we know that, but your people are very sensible and will at least give Joy a chance. Listen, and remember this when you wake up: the wolf shall also dwell with the lamb, and a little child shall lead them. Can you remember that?"

"Yes, I think so," said Bruin, and she repeated: "The wolf shall also dwell with the lamb, and a little child shall lead them."

"Good. Well, you must go now. You'll look after Joy for us. I know we can trust you – but you must trust her, too."

As he spoke these last words the wolf's voice seemed closer though he got further away and grew even larger, or, rather, Bruin got smaller and smaller, until she could see nothing but a huge, light grey cloud which folded around her, making her feel warm and cosy. When she woke up, she found herself curled up in a little ball in the middle of her bed with all the bedclothes over her head. As soon as she realised where she was she tried to remember the phrase the wolf had taught her.

It had, of course, gone completely out of her mind.

*   *   *

It was two very rattled Bailiffs that arrived at the palace later that morning round about elevenses time. Joy was not with them.

"Oh dear! Oh dear!" was all they could say to begin with.

The king and queen took them into the living room and sat them both down with large cups of tea and a plate of chocolate cake each. They knew there was no point in trying to hurry things.

"Oh, Bruin, we're so sorry," said Bailiff Right at last. "She ran off !"

Bruin's heart sank.

"Ran off," continued Bailiff Right, "after ..."

She stopped. Bailiff Left finished for her.

"... after a flock of sheep!"

Bruin's heart sank about as far as it could sink. She tried to say something but could only manage a sob, which was quickly followed by tears.

King Clovis looked from Bailiffs to daughter to wife and back to Bailiffs. "Er ... um ... could one of you ... er ... explain what all of you are ... um ... talking about ... or ... er ... crying about?" He was thoroughly puzzled.

"Oh dear!" said Bailiff Right. "Oh dear! I really must stop saying 'Oh dear!' It's this wolf, King Clovis: your daughter found a wolf yesterday and – "

"A WOLF!" bellowed the king so violently that his moustache stood bolt upright and quivered. "A WOLF did you say? On the island? Here? A WOLF you said?"

"Oh dear! Yes, I did," said the Bailiff, as though she did not really want to admit it.

"Come, come, Clovis," said the queen, who did not at all like the way her husband's moustache was behaving. "A wolf – not some wolves – she mentioned only one, you know."

"One wolf – two wolves – two hundred wolves – it's all the same. It's bad news – and it's after sheep, you say?"

"Well, she ran off towards some sheep," said Bailiff Right, who, it has to be said, remembered all too well that she had actually said "after".

"Towards – after – why is everyone being so pernickety today. Sounds to me like we've got wolves chasing sheep all over the island. We haven't got time to quibble over words. We must warn the farmers."

The king was jumping out of his chair when Bruin cried out, "No!"

He stopped, suspended half-way between standing and sitting. His moustache wavered, too, between the vertical and the horizontal. He looked at his daughter.

"Don't do that, please, daddy – they might shoot her."

Bruin fumbled for her handkerchief to dry her eyes. "She was lost. I wanted to adopt her."

"Oh, my dear," said her father, sitting down in his chair again, and sounding altogether more like his usual self as his moustache settled back to its normal position. "I'm afraid that's not on. It wouldn't do for us to be seen keeping a wolf."

"But she was so gentle," said Bruin, "wasn't she, Bailiffs? She didn't actually chase the cats. It was them that made all the fuss."

"That's true, Bruin," said Bailiff Left, her face brightening. "And when we came down to the kitchen this morning, she was lying in the corner with a couple of cats curled up beside her – wasn't she, Right? It was as though she'd lived with cats all her life."

Suddenly Bruin jumped up and ran to her father.

"Yes, of course, and the wolf shall also dwell with the lamb – or in this case the cat. Now I understand. Daddy, let's go and find her. We must trust her. She won't hurt those lambs I'm sure. She's trying to tell us something. Don't warn the farmers yet or they might hurt her."

"The farmers might have found her already," he said, and then seeing the look on Bruin's face he added, "but don't worry – you know they won't hurt her unnecessarily."

He turned to his wife. "What do you think, Clovilde my dear?"

"Well," replied the queen, who was now much happier with the state of her husband's moustache, "We've got to go and see the farmers anyway, so we might as well take Bruin with as and see what happens. But whatever we do, we'd better do it quickly."

"Right as always, my dear," said Clovis. "Can you take us back to where you last saw her, Bailiffs?"

The Bailiffs took Clovis, Clovilde and Bruin back to the place in Horngates Lane where Karlo had first seen the butterflies.

"Here we are," said Bailiff Right. "She leapt over this stile and ran off towards a flock of sheep that was grazing up on top of the hill."

They all clambered over the stile. The field ran flat across to the woods and Bruin could see the gap in the hedge which she and her brother had gone through. To the right, though, the ground rose quite steeply. The woods ran along the bottom of this hill and disappeared behind it. They could hear the sound of confused shouting coming from over the crest of the hill.

"Oh, no! It sounds as though the farmers have found her," cried Bruin.

No sooner had she spoken, than a man appeared at the top of the hill. Seeing the group below, he ran down towards them, waving a shepherd's crook wildly in the air as he came.

"King!" he called out as he approached, "King!" (There was little formality observed in Nodd – Clovilde and Clovis were simply two people who happened to have a particular job, and like everybody else they were usually addressed by the name of that job.)

"King!" he repeated when he reached them. "What a piece of luck. It was just you I was looking after."

"Shepherd!" replied the king. "What's going on up there?"

"Ah! Most peculiar!" said the man, as he fought to get his breath back. "Most peculiar! A wolf – I'd never have believed it without I saw it with my own eyes – a wolf – and I warn't alone, neither – there was others saw the same – a wolf – blow me if I couldn't disbelieve my own eyes, though, it seems so stupid when I tell it, 'cause he's mad that trusts in the tameness of a wolf."

He stopped and stared into space for a moment as he wondered how to carry on. Bruin was frantic.

"What?" she almost shouted.

The shepherd suddenly came back from wherever he had been. "A wolf! I didn't think there were no wolves on this island, but a wolf it was as sure as daylight. Yes, this wolf just rounded up all the lambs in the flock. Warn't nothing either us or the dogs or the ewes could do about it – rounded 'em all up and hustled 'em into the Wyrd Woods as smooth as a fish."

"All your lambs?" asked Clovilde.

"All on 'em – every lamb in the flock. We gave chase through the woods, but blame me if that wolf and the lambs harn't turned into bushes and trees for all we can see on 'em, Either that or butterflies, for the wood was full of butterflies, and that arn't natural for this time of year, neither."

"Butterflies!" said Bruin, excitedly. She felt hopeful for the first time since the Bailiffs had arrived with their news.

"Nothing but," said the shepherd. "We sent for more chaps and some guns, but I doubt we'll find nothing but a pile of bones and some lambs' tails – all covered in butterflies, I'll hazard."

Suddenly Bruin remembered the rest of what the big wolf had said to her in the dream: a little child shall lead them.

"Listen," she said. "I'll find the wolf, but you must promise not to hurt her if things turn out the way I say they will. Please, daddy, will you make them?"

"It's not for me to make people do anything against their better judgements, my dear, but we can ask," replied Clovis, turning to the shepherd.

"Well, much depends on what's happened to our lambs. What are you proposing, young miss?"

"It's very simple," said Bruin. "I'll go into the woods, find the wolf and the missing lambs, and bring them out here safe and sound. If the lambs are all there, unharmed, then I get to keep the wolf and look after her – is that a deal?"

"Shepherd," said Bailiff Left, "this is no ordinary wolf. I think you can trust Bruin. You and your flocks have nothing to fear."

"Very well," replied the shepherd. "I'll trust young Bruin and your wisdom, Bailiff – at least, as far as we can see the wolf – and at any road, there arn't no harm in trying, since we can't find so much as a hair off the animals' ears in them woods. I'll get everyone down here." And without further ado, he made his way back up the hill.

"Well, Bruin, I hope you know what you're doing," said her mother.

"I think so," said Bruin, and she set off towards the gap in the hedge which they had gone through the day before.

She had just gone into the woods when the shepherd reappeared at the top of the hill with about a dozen other men. They made their way down to where Clovis, Clovilde and the Bailiffs were standing. At almost exactly the same moment as they arrived, Bruin stepped back out of the woods. Around her fluttered a veil of the tiny butterflies, behind her trotted Joy, and behind Joy a line of lambs skipped and danced their way across the field.

The strange procession soon reached the group of astonished adults.

"How many lambs did you have, shepherd?" Bruin asked.

"Thirty-seven," came the reply.

"And how many can you see here?"

The shepherd counted the lambs several times over until he was quite sure.

"Well, blame me," he exclaimed at last. "No doubt about it –thirty-seven!"

"Have I won my wolf?" asked Bruin.

"I should think you have," came a chorus of reply from the shepherds.

Joy jumped up and put her paws on Bruin's shoulders, licking her face and neck. The girl held the wolf tight, tears of happiness streaming down her face. Clovilde and Clovis looked on.

"Well, come along then, my dear," said the her father to Bruin, "you'd better be getting home and show that wolf where it's going to be living from now on. Your mother and I'll just have a word with the shepherds and follow on shortly."

Bruin, Joy and the Bailiffs set off up the lane back to the palace. As soon as they got there they went straight to the kitchen, where Joy sat in the middle of the floor, head cocked slightly to one side, looking expectantly at Bruin.

"Yes, I suppose you're hungry, aren't you?" said the girl. "But I don't suppose we've got any wolf food in at the moment. What can I give you?"

"We found cat food went down very well," suggested Bailiff Right.

Bruin opened a cupboard. "Okay – what have we got? Duck, chicken, tuna, chicken with tuna, sardine and mackerel, beef, beef with kidney, duck with heart, rabbit, turkey, lamb ... ah – " she turned and looked at Joy " – maybe not lamb?"

The wolf lifted her muzzle towards the ceiling. "Uuoooowwwwwwww!" she howled – and smiled the smile of a wolf

The Treasure Hunt

The Bailiffs were so excited that they did not stop to clear up the breakfast things. In fact, they even left a teapot on the table which still had some tea in it. No sooner had they finished the muffins than they went straight to the Tomes Room, took a sheet of paper and pen each and started scribbling furiously.

The cause of this excitement was, of course, a dream - or rather, two dreams. As always over breakfast, the two Bailiffs had told each other their dreams of the previous night, and this morning they had discovered to their amazement that they seemed to have had the same dream – or at least, two halves of the same dream. Bailiff Left had dreamed that she was reading a page, but could see only the left hand side of it. Bailiff Right had dreamed that she was also reading a page, but could see only the right hand side.

"The big question is," said Right, "were we looking at the same page?"

Luckily the Bailiffs had, as no doubt you will recall, the most extraordinary memories, so they could both still remember the words they had read on their pages.

"But you know what dreams are like," said Bailiff Left. "They can slip out of your mind when you're not looking, and then run away and hide where you can never find them again. I think we ought to go and write down what we read straight away, just in case, don't you think?"

"Quite right, Left," agreed Right. "And who knows – we might even find there's more to this dream than meets the eye."

So there they were at their desks, writing as though they were in an exam.

"Right," said Left, after a couple of minutes of writing, "I'm finished. Here we are."

She took her sheet over to her friend's desk. "The only thing is, there are a couple of words that don't look … I don't know … quite what I would have expected, but I'm absolutely sure this is what I read in the dream."

"Yes, I know what you mean," said Right, taking Left's sheet and putting it down beside hers. "I had the same feeling, but I'm sure, too, that this is exactly what I dreamed."

The two women studied what they had written.

"Humph!" said Left. "Just what I thought – "

Our revels now are ended.   These our actors
As I foretold you,   were all spirit
Are melted into air.   into thin air.
And, like the baseless.   fabric of this vision,
The cloud-capped towers, the ous palaces,
The solemn temples,   the great globe itself,
Yea, all which it inherit   shall dis
And, like   insubstantial   ant faded,
Leave not a rack behind.   We are
                                and our little life

Is rounded with a sleep.

"– it's a speech from that Shakespeare
chappy's play, The Tempest."

"That's what I'd thought, as well," said
Right. "But it isn't quite all there, is it? Look –
there must be something missing after 'spirit',
because the next line doesn't make sense, then
there seems to be a whole line missing down at the
bottom here. And what on earth are 'ous palaces' –
or an 'insubstantial ant' when it's at home?"

"Well, there's only one way to find out,"
said Left, and she got up and went to a shelf from
which she took a great thick book – the complete
works of William Shakespeare. "Let's look it up
and compare our version with what's in here."

They very soon had the passage. Left rapidly copied it out on another sheet of paper and put it beside the other two sheets on Right's desk.

"Ho-ho!" exclaimed Right, as she looked from one to the other. "This is very interesting." And she started to underline some of the words, muttering to herself as she worked and getting increasingly excited.

"Yes, of course … Oh, good heavens, should've seen that one … Ah, this is beginning to make some sense…"

Very soon, she had this.

Our revels now are ended. These our actors,
As I foretold you, were all spirit<u>s and</u>
Are melted into air, into thin air.
And, like the baseless fabric of this vision,
The cloud-capped towers, the <u>gorge</u>ous palaces,
The solemn temples, the great globe itself,
Yea, all which it inherit shall dis<u>solve</u>,
And, like <u>this</u> insubstantial <u>page</u>ant faded,
Leave not a rack behind. We are <u>such stuff</u>
<u>As dreams are made on</u>, and our little life
Is rounded with a sleep.

At this moment the doorbell rang and Bailiff Left went to see who it was. She came back into the room with Bruin and Karlo. Joy the wolf followed along behind, greeting all the Bailiffs' cats as she went with a gentle poke in the rump with her muzzle.

"Just come and look," Left was saying as she ushered the children in. "I really think we're on to something."

Bruin and Karlo stood behind Right's chair and craned over, eager to see what the Bailiffs were making such a fuss about.

"Yes," said Right, "there's definitely a message here – do you see?"

The children looked even harder at the page of scribble, then at each other with 'what on earth are they talking about' looks on their faces, and then at Bailiff Left who was almost hopping up and down with excitement.

"Oh my elbows! Yes! I see what you mean – 'sand gorge, solve this page, we are such stuff as dreams are made on.' Well, we'd better be going, then. Shall I pack up a picnic?"

"I should think so," replied Right. "Are you two game for a picnic in Sand Gorge?" she asked the children.

Sand Gorge was one of the most beautiful beaches on the island of Nodd, and a picnic there was something they could understand, so this suggestion was greeted with an enthusiastic chorus of 'yesses' and 'you bets'.

"We'd better send Joy back with a note for Mum and Dad," said Bruin. "Then she can meet us at the gorge later. But won't you explain what this is all about? We're completely lost!" "Oh, it's all very simple, really," said Left. "But we'll do it on the way. Let's get the picnic packed up first."

*   *   *

"So what does all that Bakesbeer stuff mean, then?" asked Karlo, as they walked along the coast path high above the sea. "I couldn't make head or tail of it when you showed it to us back at your house."

"Shakespeare, Karlo, not 'Bakesbeer,'" corrected Bailiff Right, "and it's quite true that it's not easy to understand, and luckily it doesn't really matter what this passage means – it's the message in it for us that we need to work out."

"That's a relief," thought Karlo, who did not really go much for poetry and that sort of stuff. But his relief was short lived, because the Bailiff carried on.

"But to put it in a nutshell, this is a speech from a play called The Tempest. At one point the main character, a magician called Prospero, stages a show for two other characters – that's what 'our revels' means, a play – and this show is performed by spirits under his magical command. When the actor-spirits have disappeared, he says to the two characters that the real world around us is in fact just as unreal as the play they have just seen, and will also vanish away one day – dissolve, leaving not so much as a cloud behind."

"That's what a 'rack' is," put in Left, "a cloud."

"In other words," carried on Right, "our life is just a dream, and on either side of it is sleep – that sort of sleep when you are just unconscious, and not dreaming."

"Sounds a bit dismal when you put it like that," said Bruin. "I thought it sounded rather lovely, that line – 'we are such stuff as dreams are made on.' But why 'on'? I don't get that."

"Ah, yes, actually, it means 'of' here – 'we are the stuff of dreams,' I suppose you could say."

"Why doesn't he say that, then?" complained Karlo. "Why can't he write in plain language?"

"Well, to start with," explained Right, "our language was slightly different when Shakespeare was writing – language changes all the time, you know. And then again, that's poetry for you – it's a bit of a challenge to the mind. That's the fun of it, I suppose. But anyway, as I said, it's the way we dreamed it that enabled us to work out that message – go to Sand Gorge and work out the clue on this page."

"But you know why Sand Gorge is famous, don't you?" asked Left.

"It's where that pirate, Captain Granguzzle, came ashore after he was shipwrecked on Proboscis Point," said Karlo, who was a bit more up on the history of piracy.

"That's right. And oddly enough, The Tempest starts with a shipwreck. Now," said Left, "doesn't that make it look as though this is a message from Granguzzle?"

"Gosh! I see!" cried Karlo, suddenly much more excited. "You mean this is a clue to where he buried his treasure!"

"Well, that's one possibility," said the Bailiff, with a smile.

"Oh, wow!" shouted Karlo, jumping up in the air. "We're going to find pirate treasure! Let me see that Shakesbeard thing again!"

"Shakespeare!" said Right, with a little exasperation in her voice. She handed the sheet to Karlo and he began to study it with unaccustomed concentration.

"So who was this Captain Granguzzle, then?" asked Bruin.

"He used to operate around these islands about two hundred and fifty years ago," replied

Bailiff Left, "and he was a bit of an odd fish – for a pirate, at any rate. You see, he was never known to have actually taken anything from another ship that he seized – all he did was demand a meal from the captain of the captured ship"

"And he'd settle for nothing less than five courses – with a good wine," added Right.

"You see," continued Left, "he had an enormous nose and with it an astonishing sense of smell. He could smell any ship that had good food on board from miles away and as soon as he had sniffed out a likely victim he would have his flag run up the main mast – "

" His flag was a skillet and cross spoons which he called the Jolly Nosher," put in Bailiff Right.

" – and send out a boarding party to inform the captain that he was 'about to receive a guest' as Granguzzle put it. Apparently, he was searching for something, something in the edible line, that is, but if anyone ever asked him what, he'd come over all mysterious and say something like, 'That, sir, is a good deal more than I am permitted to reveal,' and then burst out laughing."

"Because the other thing about him was that he was a great joker," continued Bailiff Right. "Whilst he was gorging himself at his host's table, his men would distract the captive crew somehow or other, whilst the women – and there were as many women as men in his crew – set about some mischief on the ship. Once, they put a different kind of reptile in every hammock – nothing poisonous, mind you, just something wriggly or slimy. Another time, they switched the maps in the chart room for a new lot which were perfectly accurate but upside down. When the captain of the ship came back from dinner to check his position, he thought Granguzzle's crew had turned his ship round – "

" – so of course he turned it round," said Left, "and sailed back to where he'd come from!"

"I suppose he came to a bad end, like all pirates," said Bruin, sadly.

"No, actually he didn't," said Left. "After he was shipwrecked he gave up piracy and spent the rest of his life studying flowers. In fact, he wrote a book on the flowers of the islands – very good it is, too."

"But how come," asked Karlo, "he got rich enough to have any treasure to bury if he never stole anything?"

"That was as great a mystery then as it is now," replied Bailiff Right. "But rich he was, and staggeringly so, it was said, and I suppose he must have been, because apart from anything else it must have cost a small fortune to keep his own ship at sea. Some said he did his plundering in the western oceans, not liking to steal from his own country folk. Others maintained that he did it under a different name long before he started his peculiar culinary quest. Yet another story was that he was simply an extremely rich eccentric who had nothing better to do – piracy was just a bit of fun. But even though he was completely harmless, any captain who heard the look-out cry, "Avast below! The Jolly Nosher!" would feel his heart sink to his boots, knowing that his ship's larder was about to be raided for all its choicest morsels, and he was about to become the victim of some foolish practical joke."

"Oh well," said Karlo, "at least it sounds like he must have had some treasure on board when he was shipwrecked at Sand Gorge."

"Yes," agreed Bailiff Left. "And here we are."

And indeed, just at that moment, as they went over the crest of the hill they saw the track plunge into a deep rocky valley, the floor of which was covered with pure white sand. Their path led straight on to the sand, which broadened out into a magnificent beach as it sloped gently down to the sea. To the left and right of this beach the valley sides ran into the sea, the one on the left ending about fifty metres out in a final thrust of dark, jagged rocks, the fearsome Proboscis Point on which poor Granguzzle had come to grief.

The party headed for the only shade in the gorge, a clump of gnarled, sea-beaten trees about halfway down the beach that seemed to be crouching for shelter behind an outcrop of rock. That was also the only vegetation they could see in the whole of Sand Gorge, apart from a vivid patch of frothy yellow flowers about twenty metres up the side of the valley exactly opposite the trees.

"There's Joy!" cried Bruin, spotting her pet who was already there, sitting in the shade.

"Good heavens!" said Bailiff Left. "That wolf doesn't hang about, does she?"

Joy ran out to meet them. She had a roll of paper in her mouth which she gave to Bruin.

"Good wolf," said the girl, taking the paper. She read out the message. "Thank you for note received by wolf 12.13 p.m.. Ours herewith by return wolf. Have a nice picnic. Please be home by 6.00 p.m. at latest. Regards to Bailiffs. Father."

"Splendid!" said Right. "Let's sit down and have that picnic, then, while we consider our next move."

"And we can enjoy looking at that beautiful patch of flowers up there," said Left, as she unpacked her ruck-sack on to the sand. "The name of it escapes me for the moment, but it'll come back before long."

* * *

Lunch over, they lay in the shade enjoying the warm summer air and the lazy sound of the sea washing gently on the shore.

"'We are such stuff as dreams are made on,'" repeated Karlo. "I could do some dreaming right now. I wonder if I'd dream the answer to the clue?"

Suddenly Bailiff Left sat bolt upright. "You don't need to," she said. "I've got it!"

The others all sat bolt upright as well, except for Joy, who just opened one eye and raised an ear – wolves know how to save energy.

"It's Ladies' Bedstraw," said Left. They carried on looking at her. "That flower up there on the hill side. It was used for stuffing mattresses once because of its sweet scent, you know, and that's what dreams are made on, aren't they – mattresses?"

"My toenails, I think you might be right," said Right.

"So he did mean 'on' – you know, meaning 'on'?" said Karlo.

"Well, perhaps Granguzzle thought that's what it meant. But it's worth a try, anyway – let's go and look." And she led them up the hill, explaining as they went that Ladies' Bedstraw was also used to make foot-baths for weary travellers and for curdling milk in cheese making once upon a time, but the others were far too excited to take much notice.

They stood, all rather out of breath but almost laughing with anticipation, looking at the patch of tall, thin leafed stems with their delicate yellow froth of petals. The patch looked bigger than it did from below, but even then it was only about three metres in circumference.

"Oh, look! Someone must have planted these here," said Right. "That earth isn't natural. D'you see - there's not a grain of it anywhere else on this hillside."

"Shall we get Joy to dig?" said Bruin, already pushing the wolf in amongst the flowers.

"Yes – but only in the middle," said Left. "We don't want to damage them too much."

"Go on then, Joy," said Bruin, and Joy nosed her way through and started to dig.

"Hurry up!" cried Karlo. He was hopping up and down with excitement. "Oh wow! Do you think this is it? Do you think there's a chest of gold coins under there?"

"Pieces of eight! Spanish doubloons!"
laughed Bruin, as dirt, stones, and bits of flowers
flew out of the patch of Ladies' Bedstraw.

The Bailiffs tried to look very calm, but
really they were just as excited as the children and
when the sound of wolf paws scrabbling in earth
suddenly changed to that of wolf paws scraping
against wood they could hide their feelings no
longer.

"D'you hear that!" shouted Right, running
round to the other side of the patch to try and get a
better look at what Joy was doing.

"Yes!" chorused the others.

"I'm going to help her," cried Left, who
could stand the suspense no longer. She ran in
amongst the flowers and disappeared from view as
she got down on her hands and knees. Dirt and
stones began to cascade from the other side of the
patch. And then – "Oh my ears! Look at this!"

"What! What!" shouted the others. Bailiff
Left stood up. In her hands was a small wooden
sphere, about the size of a melon.

"Oh!" said Karlo, the disappointment clear in
his voice. "There can't be much gold in there."

"Don't be silly," said Bruin. "Suppose it's
full of diamonds and pearls."

"Yes – yes – of course," cried Karlo, all his
hopes restored. "Or rubies and emeralds."

"Sapphires and amethysts," added Bruin.

"Now then, children," said Bailiff Left as she and Joy came out from the flowers, "don't let's get too excited. It's obviously hollow, but it isn't very heavy. I'm afraid there can't be much in it – but it's very pretty. Look."

She held the sphere so that they could all see it. It was made of a dark wood, and there were patches of faded blue, green and white paint all over it.

"Do you know what?" said Bruin, who had been examining it carefully. "I think it's a globe. The green is land, the blue the sea, and the white patches are the two poles."

"There you are,'" said Left. "Don't you remember - 'the great globe itself.' It all fits in with the passage we dreamed."

Karlo groaned with disappointment. "Is that all," he said. "A manky old wooden globe!"

Bailiff Right put a hand round his shoulders. "Don't give up yet, Karlo – remember that it went on to talk about inheriting the globe. Maybe there's more to it."

"And where the equator would be is a groove – do you see," carried on Bruin with mounting excitement, "like perhaps it's two halves joined together."

"Yes, so it is," said Karlo, his enthusiasm coming back, "Can you open it, Bailiff Left?"

The Bailiff put one hand on each of the poles and twisted them in opposite directions. Nothing happened. She tried again, still without success. Bailiff Right took the globe and tried, but she had no more luck.

"Give it to me – I'll break it open," said Karlo. "Crack – like a coconut." He mimed hurling it to the ground.

"No, Karlo, certainly not!" protested Bailiff Right. "This is probably Captain Granguzzle's globe – it's a piece of our history, and it's survived over two hundred years of lying in the earth. We're not having you smash it to pieces in a couple of seconds."

Karlo looked disappointed.

"Besides," continued the Bailiff, "suppose it were completely empty – we'd feel a right bunch of idiots. No, we must use our brains – they've got us this far, I've no doubt they'll get us into this."

"Perhaps it's jammed up with earth," suggested Bruin. "You could try just gently tapping it against a rock. I've seen people do that with things that are stuck."

Right knocked the globe a few times very gingerly against a nearby rock, then tried twisting again. To whoops of delight from everybody the two hemispheres turned easily and came apart.

"There – that's what using your brain does," she said, looking rather pointedly in Karlo's direction. However, like everybody else, he was too interested in what was inside the globe to notice.

"What's in it, Bailiff, show us what's in it?" he begged.

Bailiff Right carefully lifted the northern hemisphere off and looked into the southern one. The others watched her face, but it revealed nothing.

And indeed, that is precisely what was in the globe – nothing. It was as empty as a bottomless bucket. The Bailiff held the two halves upside down and gave them a good shake.

"Nothing!" she said.

"Nothing?" echoed Karlo.

"Nothing!" repeated Bailiff Right.

She turned the hemispheres over and peered into them with her one eye to check, first the south, and then the north. But then, suddenly, her eye lit up. "Just a moment, though!" She peered closer, "there's something on the inside surface of this one." She looked more carefully at the other. "And in this one, too. Do you see, Left?"

Bailiff Left peered in, and sure enough, she could see several lines of faint but very neat writing. "Yes – it looks like lines of poetry."

"Oh no!" groaned Karlo. "Not more Makesweird."

Bailiff Right knew when she was being baited, so she did not try to correct Karlo this time. Instead she gave him the two halves of the globe. "Here's a nice little job for you," she said with the hint of a smile. "You can work out what's written in these."

Karlo' face fell. "But it's poetry!" he complained.

"Oh, come on, Karlo – I'll help you," said Bruin, taking one of the hemispheres from him. "You never know – it might be another clue."

Karlo could see the sense of this. "Okay," he said, "but it's too hot up here. Let's go back down into the shade."

"Good idea," said Left. "We'll try to put things a bit back to rights here while you two do that."

"And perhaps that wolf could sort out a drink for us all," added Right, though it has to be said she did not really hold out much hope on that score.

When the Bailiffs got back to the picnic spot Bruin was still poring over her hemisphere, whilst her brother was just sitting and looking dejectedly out towards the sea.

"Oh dear, Karlo, can't you make anything of it?" asked Left.

"We know what it says," he replied in a tired voice. "But it's another stupid poem, and it doesn't make any sense at all." His hopes had been raised and dashed so many times since they had started that he was beginning to lose heart.

"It's a riddle," said Bruin, looking up. "I've got the second and the fifth letters, but the others are a bit tricky."

"A riddle!" exclaimed Right. "We love riddles, don't we Left? Let's hear it."

So the two children read out their halves of the globe, Bruin starting:

"My first is a sound that you'll hear in a shell.
My second's the gateway to heaven and hell.
My third and my fourth and my sixth are the same
As the second in second – oh my, what a game!
The letter that's left you will find with some ease,
A twister and snaky – it's in both of these."

Then Karlo picked up his half and read rather wearily:

"And when I'm the colour of sky or of sea
There's nothing at all, whether costly or free,
Can give human beings a tenth of the pleasure.
Now that's what a sensible person calls treasure.

If you can work out what is meant by this puzzle
You'll learn what was prized most by Captain
Granguzzle."

The Bailiffs thought for a moment, then
looked at one another. For obvious reasons they
could not wink, though had they been able to do so
they might have done just that. As it was, they
simply burst out laughing.

"So," said Left, "the first clue was made of
what we had dreamt – it was quite literally the
stuff that our dreams were made of!"

" And the second clue," added Right, "was
for him what he treasured most in his dreams of
culinary pleasure. Well, I told you Granguzzle was
famous for his practical jokes, didn't I?"

"Never mind," said Left. "It gave us a good
excuse for a picnic, and we've had a bit of fun.
What more could we ask?"

Suddenly, Bruin fell on her back and let out
a theatrical groan. "Oh, no – I get it now! Is that
all!" she cried.

"I wish someone would tell me what's going
on," complained the bewildered Karlo, looking
from Bruin to Bailiffs and back again. "What is the
answer to this stupid riddle?"

"Come now, Karlo, you wouldn't want us to
deprive you of the pleasure of working it out for
yourself, would you?" asked Right.

"No," said Left, "that wouldn't be fair, would it Bruin?"

"Oh no," agreed his sister. "That's all the fun of a riddle."

"Well I think you're all really mean," sulked Karlo. "And as for that stupid Granguzzle … "

"Here," said Bailiff Right, passing him a plate, "have the last sandwich as a consolation prize."

"What's in it?" asked Karlo suspiciously.

The Bailiff peeked under the bread. "Stilton and lettuce," she said.

Karlo perked up. "Blue cheese? Oh, that's my favourite!" And he bit hungrily into the sandwich – but he never did understand why the other three laughed so uproariously.

Dream On

It was half past eight in the morning when Karlo, bleary eyed, staggered down to breakfast. He fell into a chair, where he managed to open his eyes sufficiently to look at the breakfast table. After a moment, he became aware that he was being watched. An almost magnetic power drew his attention to the other end of the table, from which his father, Clovis, studied him.

"Good morning, Karlo," said Clovis, rather sternly (when you are a king you are, of course expected to speak sternly). "School holidays, I know, but a little on the late side, aren't we, hm? Why would that be?"

"Because he's a lazy boy," whispered Bruin to her wolf, Joy, as she passed the animal a bit of toast. Then she corrected herself. "No – actually it's because he's a boy."

"Yes, dad, sorry ... well ... it's sort of ... it's just that I was having such a good dream."

"All well and good," said Clovis, in a slightly more friendly voice. "I'm pleased to hear you have good dreams, but you can't dream your breakfast. The egg will be hard by now, I don't doubt, and the toast cold – that's no way to start the day. Now you can't afford ..."

Karlo poured some cornflakes into a bowl, and let the all-too familiar lecture on the benefits of a good breakfast wash over him as the milk washed over his cereal. It was so well known as to be almost comforting, and it began to have much the same effect as a favourite bed-time story.

*   *   *

"But just think of it, Bruin," he said to his sister. "You don't need to eat breakfast in dreams – in fact, you don't need to eat at all. There's all sorts of things you don't have to do – or if you do dream something really awful, like that you're at school, you pretty soon sort of dream out of it. Dreaming is so good."

He lay back on the grass and looked at the sky where the clouds made soft shapes to dream on.

"Look at that one, Bruin – it's almost the shape of a camel."

"No, I think it's like a weasel!" teased his sister.

"Or like a whale!"

"Oh yes, very like a whale! Karlo, you are such a lazy boy!"

98

"No, it's not because I like sleeping – I like dreaming. It's different," insisted Karlo. "Don't you? Don't you love that moment before going to sleep when everything goes sort of woozy, then your mind like slips from under you just when you aren't looking and you're into the dream world? Why can't I live in that world?"

"Like a whale! Like a big cloudy whale!" sang Bruin, who hadn't listened to a word he had said.

Karlo sat up and looked out to sea. "Yes, like a whale," he said, "like a singing whale in a sea of dream."

"But what if you never woke up?"

"I wouldn't want to wake up, That's the whole point. Why would I ever want to wake up?"

Bruin looked rather worried at this idea. "You'd miss your birthday, and what's more, you'd end up not knowing whether you were asleep or awake. That's silly."

"Oh, you don't understand, Bruin," said Karlo. Suddenly he jumped to his feet. "I know who I need to talk to. Let's go to Horngates Tower and see the Bailiffs. Come on!"

"No, it's too far for a day by the sea. I'm going to pick some weasels for breakfast," said Bruin, and she ran off into the sky.

"Girls!" scoffed Karlo. "It's only a couple of minutes."

*   *   *

Karlo whistled, and his bike, which was lying behind a sand dune, spun its back wheel and purred like a cat. "Come along, Harley, it's just you and I," said Karlo as he pedalled off down the lane.

The path, however, did not seem quite as straight as usual. This made Karlo feel a little uneasy to begin with but Harley swept smoothly round the bends and simply skimmed over the bumps and ruts and the huge stones that littered the way so that Karlo forgot his fear, abandoning himself to the wonderful sensation of flying.

On and on they flew, the bends getting sharper every second and Harley speeding even faster. Karlo discovered that his mind was now flying along about two metres above his body, and when they came to a bend that looped completely round on itself he felt no concern, just a mild curiosity as to how Harley would cope with this new challenge. The answer was simple: the bike folded itself in the middle like a pair of compasses and became a unicycle! Round the loop it spun and carried on its way as though it were on rails rather than a rough country path.

However, the road had not finished with them yet. Karlo's heart sank when he saw a tangle of bends up ahead that reminded him of nothing quite so much as a huge pile of spaghetti. Surely Harley could not get through this! But before Karlo had time to worry any longer, they were on it, in it, amongst it, Harley's single wheel gyrating crazily amongst the chaos of twists and turns, stopping, reversing and spinning off again, all in a fragment of a second. And then they were through it.

Karlo sighed with relief. "Good bike, Harley," he said, and patted its handlebars. But the road to the Bailiffs' house had never been quite like this – never so frightening but also never so exciting. He stopped the bike, got off and lay down under an elm tree growing beside the road to get his mind back.

*   *   *

As he stared up into the branches above him he became aware of something watching him. His eyes searched amongst the shelves of the tree, until he spied the robin, sitting between two large books and observing him through a telescope. The bird was actually far too big for a robin – it was more like the size of a swan, but the dumpy shape, sharp, dagger-like beak and dark orange breast left no room for doubt. It was not its size that bothered Karlo, though, so much as the fact that it looked horribly like his father, King Clovis. Indeed, the bird even had a crown on his head.

On seeing that he had been seen, the robin took the telescope away from his eye, and said, much to Karlo's surprise, "Not so much of the 'hey', if you don't mind – and even less of the 'bird'! 'Your Majesty' to you, if you please."

He then turned the telescope round and, putting it back to his eye, continued to peer at Karlo. Before he could think, Karlo had shouted out, "Hey, bird!"

The robin very carefully gripped his telescope in one claw and flew down on to a shelf on a level with Karlo's head. Here he took the instrument in one wing put it to his left eye and puffed out his chest. "I'm looking at you," he said, as though he were stating the obvious.

"Who are you looking at?" Karlo asked, again without thinking before he spoke, and then he almost kicked himself. "Drat it!" he thought. "This pesky bird is answering my questions before I've asked them. What can I do about this?"

But he did not have a chance to think before the bird said, "Because you are lost."

And almost at the same time Karlo heard himself say, "Anyway, why are you looking at me?" Again he realised that he had been tricked, and he banged on the ground with his fist in frustration.

"All right," he said to himself, "I'll play along with you for a while, King Robin, but I know your game now." And he began to think of a way in which he could outwit the bird.

"Ah!" said the Robin, "you refer, I take it, to the wonderful instrument parked at this present instant under my right wing – the Metachronic Pseudoscope."

"And what's that thing you were watching me through?" asked Karlo obediently.

"Because it sees things the opposite way round to how they happen – as, for first example," and he held up the first feather of his left wing, "one might be looking at a field that it has been harvested, and then, when you look through this instrument at the field you see the harvester at work. Or, for a second," and he held up the second feather of his left wing, "you might see a light come on in a room, then look through this instrument at that room and see someone flick a light switch on the wall. So, by this means, I can see the result of something before I see what has caused it to happen."

"Huh! There's no big deal about that," thought Karlo. "That's what detectives do, and it happens in books all the time." But he asked the necessary question, nonetheless, as he prepared to lure the robin into a trap. "And why is it called that?"

"By all means," said the bird. He handed the Pseudoscope with its two little lens caps to Karlo. "I suggest you take my first example and look at that field over there."

"May I have a look through it?" Karlo asked as he took it and put the lens caps down near him, and thought up his next question. But instead of looking at the field, he turned the instrument on the bird itself and, just as he had hoped, it was no longer on its shelf. Quick as a flash, he took the Pseudoscope from his eye, snatched up the lens caps and slipped them on the instrument.

"Oh, do you really have to go? This was just getting interesting, your majesty," said Karlo. He put his ear to the tube and smiled as he heard a muffled scrabbling and tweeting coming from inside it. Satisfied that the robin was safely bottled up, Karlo sat back feeling very pleased with himself.

However, the bird was quite right about one thing. Karlo was indeed lost, and he had no idea how this came to be. He had made the journey to Horngates Tower, the Bailiffs' house, hundreds of times, and did not remember ever having to pass through a library, especially one as large as this.

It was, in fact, huge, with a great dome full of scaffolding. The only people Karlo could see were walking around the very highest levels of the scaffolding right up in the dome, so high up that he could not tell whether they were talking or not. He lifted his head up towards the dome and shouted, "HOW DO I GET OUT OF HERE!" at the top of his voice.

There was not the slightest response to his call. The people on the scaffolding just went about their business as if he simply did not exist.

"LOOK AT ME!" he yelled at them. Not one so much as twitched an ear. "HELP ME! I'M LOST!"

Suddenly Karlo began to feel a bit worried. Perhaps they were ignoring him because he was not really there. Perhaps he did not even exist. But then he quickly comforted himself with the thought that if he did not exist then there would be nobody to be lost.

"I'm lost, therefore I am," he said to himself, and felt better immediately.

But how had he got lost in the first place? Where had he been going? And was it morning or evening, lunch time or breakfast time? And, most perplexing of all, why was the air so brown? This last question made him feel very weary – it was just one question too many.

"What I need is a nap," he thought. He looked around for a suitable dog to lie on, but there was not a dog in sight.

"But of course," he thought, "there aren't any dogs in Nodd any more – they all melted last summer. But if I could only go to sleep I could dream a dog, and then I could sleep on that dog and then I could dream my way out of here, but how can I do that when I'm so hungry?"

"You need a sandwich," said a voice behind him.

Karlo swung round. There was no-one there – just two flat, oblong shaped pieces of wood leaning against one another so that they made a kind of tent shape, or an upside down V. On the top edge where they joined together there were two loops of stiff material that stood up, and on the side facing him was written in a strange, dark script:

Nothing
Is
Better

He had seen something like this before in a book, but there it had been hung over the shoulders of a man who carried it around as a kind of walking advertisement and because the man was sandwiched between the two boards it was called a sandwich board.

"Perhaps," thought Karlo, "the man is inside, or behind it."

When he walked round it to look, though, there was no sign of any person at all – but the message was different:

Nothing

Is

Best

"Is there somebody there?" he asked.

"Of course there is – can't you see what you're looking at?" said a rather irritable voice, which clearly came out of the wooden tent.

"Who are you?" asked Karlo, still puzzled about who exactly was talking to him.

"I'm Board – Sandwich Board – at your service," came the voice.

"Oh!" said Karlo. "So what do you do?"

"Nothing much," came the reply. "That's why I'm bored."

"I thought you said 'Board'," said Karlo.

"I did," said Board.

"But that's not the same as 'bored' – it's spelt differently – it's a different word," insisted Karlo.

"What's the difference?" asked Board rather sharply. "It's the same sound – same sound, same noise. Just a noise – like you."

"What do you mean, like me?"

"What I said," shouted Board, who began hopping up and down and flapping his front and back together in sheer frustration. "Just annoys – asking all these silly questions!"

"You're doing it again," protested Karlo.

"Doing what?" demanded Board.

"Using a word with a different spelling, then pretending it's the same one. You said 'a noise' first and then pretended you'd said 'annoys'. Different spelling, different word." Karlo was getting quite irritated himself.

"Same noise, same word," persisted Board. "
"That's all words are – noises. I'll prove it – listen: just say any word over and over to yourself and after a while it changes back into what it really is – just a noise. Go on – try it. Say 'sandwich' to yourself over and over again – 'sandwich

sandwich sandwich sand witch sand widge sand widge san dwidge ... see – what does that mean?"

Karlo was not at all convinced. "It doesn't matter how you spell it – it still sounds the same, so ..."

"Isn't that just what I've been saying all along," crowed Sandwich Board triumphantly. "Now maybe you'll stop arguing."

But Karlo was not going to stop. "But if it is just a noise, then it doesn't mean anything, so it can't be a word because a word is a noise that means something, and what's more, you're called Sandwich, so if that's just a noise that means you're meaningless."

"You're meaning-less," said Board. "You're meaning less and less every time you open your mouth!"

"Prove it!" shouted Karlo, who was getting really angry with this stupid piece of wood.

"Nothing easier," replied Board, giggling to himself. "You just said 'that means you're meaningless' – yes?"

"Yes," agreed Karlo.

"Well how can anything 'mean what's meaningless'? You might as well say that meaning hasn't got any meaning. You might as well say it isn't what it is – or even that it is what it isn't."

Then, suddenly changing the subject before Karlo could get in a reply, he said, "Do you want to get out of here or not?"

Karlo lay flat on his back. Mean ... meaning ... meaningless – the words were flopping around in his mind like great white ghosts and, to his horror, they had become just sounds, empty noises, exactly as Board claimed words did when you said them too much. He was beginning to wonder if there were any words left in his head that meant anything at all.

"Just at the moment," he said, "I'd like nothing better."

"Oh! 'Like nothing better'?" repeated Board. "In other words, you'd rather have nothing ... ?"

Karlo sighed wearily. "Well, that's not quite what I meant ..."

"Well it's what you said and it's what you ought to have meant because that's just what you need. I do wish people would say what I want them to mean and mean what I want them to say!" Board was hopping up and down again in a terrible flap. "Now then, let's start again – you want to get out of here but you'd rather have nothing and that's just as well because nothing is exactly what you need."

At this point Board fell flat on its face. Karlo thought this was just part of the tantrum, but then he saw that Board had turned into a tray, on which lay a plate with a piece of bread on it – or at least, the remains of a piece of bread. The entire middle had been very neatly taken out of it, so that all that was left was the crust.

"Here," said Board's voice, sounding rather muffled as though it was coming from underneath the tray, "have a Nothing Sandwich!"

Karlo looked at the crust for a few moments, not sure what to do or say. The tray trembled slightly and Board's voice, muffled but still clearly irritated, came from underneath it.

"Go on – what are you waiting for? Get through it!"

"I'm ... er ... not sure ... do you mean eat it?" asked Karlo.

"Of course not!" came the reply. "You can't eat nothing – you might as well eat air for all the good that would do you! No – pick it up and get through it, boy, get through it!"

Karlo was quite bewildered by this peculiar instruction, but rather than risk annoying Board any further he picked up the crust and held it to his face.

"The trouble is, it's a bit small," he said.

"Nonsense! You haven't even tried yet. What you're holding is the trap door of the Dream World. Just say where you want to be in your dreams and clamber through – you'll be there. Go on!"

Board's voice no longer sounded angry but encouraging, and this made Karlo more willing to try. He put both his hands inside the square of crust and pulled slightly. To his surprise, the soft bread did not give way. Instead, he felt himself pulled closer to the hole. With a little more effort he pulled his head through the crust and found himself peering into a familiar room as though he was entering it through a trap door. It was the living room of Horngates Tower, and there, sure enough, were the two Bailiffs themselves, sitting in their familiar places, Right on the right of Left and Left on the left of Right. (This was how they always sat unless they were quarrelling with one another, in which case they swapped sides which they did so that they could glare at one another more closely, each with her one good eye. You could tell when they had made up their quarrel because they returned to their normal positions. Luckily for the cats which invariably occupied their laps, they did not quarrel very often or for very long, but they had been known, on a bad day, to change places up to twenty-four times.)

"Ah! Bailiffs! You're just the people I want to see," said Karlo, climbing out of the crust. "What a relief!"

"What a surprise!" said Bailiff Right.

"So, what's the problem?" asked Left.

"Well ..." said Karlo, then paused. He was still feeling very confused.

"Come and sit down," said Right, "and have a cat – there's nothing better to help you collect your thoughts together."

As Karlo got into one of the big, comfy armchairs a black cat jumped onto his lap and immediately he remembered why he was there.

"It all started when I was thinking that in dreams, you don't need to eat breakfast – that you don't need to eat at all, and that got me thinking about all the other things you don't have to do in dreams, like going to school or tidying up your room. And so I thought, why can't I just live in a dream – you know, move in to it, like you do into a new house. t would be such fun. Then I remembered that you two know all about dreams, don't you, and you're always saying that dreaming is good for you."

"Oh, yes, it certainly is," said Bailiff Right. "The history of Nodd is full of stories about people who have been helped by dreams."

"Not to mention dreams of people that have been helped by stories," added Left.

"No, or of stories of dreams that have been helped by people," said Right.

"Or of helping stories that are peopled with dreams," said Left.

"Or dreaming stories that are peopled with help," said Right.

Karlo, head was swinging from one to the other as though he was watching a tennis match. He was beginning to think it might start spinning round and round when luckily they stopped.

"Well then, why can't we live in our dreams all the time?" he asked.

Bailiff Left studied her toes. On one, she could just make out the shape of a tiny butterfly.

"I am reminded," she said, "by one of my toes, of So-Shu."

"Ah, yes," said Right, "quite so."

"Yes, quite So-Shu," replied Left. "He was a man of great learning who lived in a country called China about two hundred years ago. He once dreamt that he was a butterfly, and on waking asked himself whether So-Shu had just dreamt he was a butterfly, or whether in fact he was a butterfly that was now dreaming it was So-Shu. This puzzled him for many years."

"And did he ever find an answer?" asked Karlo.

"In a way, yes," replied Bailiff Left. "Reasoning that, if he was a butterfly, he could fly, one day he jumped off a hillock in a cow field" (here she flapped her arms and for a moment became a huge, vividly coloured pair of wings) "and fell flat on his face in a cow pat!"

Karlo laughed. "I reckon that proved he was a man."

"Yes – or that butterflies can't fly in their sleep," put in Bailiff Right.

"One might also learn another lesson: don't practise flying in a cow field," added Left, joining in the laughter. "But truly, it's not always easy to tell where dreaming ends and real life begins. You must simply learn to trust your dreams to tell you. Dream on, Karlo, dream on. It can only do you good."

Bailiff Right handed him a glass. "And drink up your Snail Crush – that's good for you, too."

Karlo took the tumbler of dirty green, frothy looking liquid, rather reluctantly it has to be said, but he was too polite to refuse. As he tipped it up to drink he felt the sharp, crisp fragments of broken snail shell tickle his nose and the gluey liquid brush his lips. For some reason the Bailiffs had started talking about breakfast – they sounded just like his father – and the cat had climbed on to his face, making it difficult for him to breathe.

For a moment, things seemed entirely not right, then Karlo realised that he actually was at the breakfast table, flopped over it and his face in his bowl of cereal. With a start he sat up and looked around him through a mask of soggy cornflakes.

Everyone was staring at him, his parents with some concern, and his sister with barely successful attempts to control her laughter.

"Are you well, dear?" asked his mother.

"Yes ... yes ... fine ..." spluttered Karlo through the cornflakes, which flew off all over the table. "But a bit hungry – need a good breakfast. Pass the muffins, please, Bruin."

When he took the basket his sister handed to him it felt strangely heavy. Karlo peered into it.

There, enjoying each others' company, were five furry weasels. (Or were they stoats?)

Surprise Surprise!

"Karlo?"

"Bruin?"

"Do you remember what's happening in a fortnight's time?"

"Er … um … well … well … er – actually, no!"

"Oh, you are hopeless!"

"Well don't go on at me – tell me – what is happening in a fortnight's time?"

"It's mummy and daddy's birthday – their *fortieth* birthday!"

"Oh! Are they really that old?"

"That's not the point!"

"So what is the point?"

"Oh, you are hopeless! The point is that we ought to do something special to help them celebrate it."

"Like what?"

"We ought to organise something for them."

"Like what?"

"Like a surprise party."

"Oh yes – a party – what a good idea!"

This last comment resolved what was in danger of becoming a rather fractious conversation which could have cast a cloud over the bright summer morning that found the twins Bruin and Karlo, with, of course, Joy the wolf, on their way to have lunch at Horngates Tower.

"We could ask the Bailiffs if they have any other ideas," suggested Bruin.

"Yes, they're good at ideas," replied Karlo. "They're so brainy."

"Unlike some brothers I know," thought Bruin, but in the interests of maintaining harmony she kept the thought to herself.

*   *   *

Lunch over they repaired to the living room of Horngates Tower and the big comfy chairs that were permanently covered in cats. Joy nosed some cats to the edges of the chairs so that Bruin and Karlo could sit down.

"Well," started Bailiff Left, "what is this that you wanted to talk to us about?"

Bruin knew better than to ask how the Bailiff knew that she had something particular to discuss with them, so she went straight to the point.

"On July 14th, as you know, it will be our parents' fortieth birthdays, and we thought that we ought to do something a bit special to celebrate it – didn't we Karlo? "she added with one of those looks at her brother. "But so far we haven't got much further than the idea of throwing a party, but just a party doesn't seem special enough, so we thought that talking to you about this would give us a few other ideas to choose from."

"Okay, then," said Bailiff Right without more ado, "let's brainstorm – off we go!"

So off they went ….

"A picnic at Sand Gorge … what if it rains? … too much trouble getting all the food there … sand in the sandwiches …not enough room … perform a play … which one? … 'Beauty and the Beast' … I'll be the beauty – you can be the beast … look who's talking … too much additional work, have to build a set … not to mention make costumes … and learn lines … a concert of music … I don't play any instruments … get in professionals … how would we pay them? … okay, drop that … a fancy dress ball … we'd need a theme … not enough time to make costumes … and same problem with musicians … a magic lantern show … the last one wasn't exactly a roaring success … wasn't my fault … humph …hide and seek in the shrubbery … or build a maze and all get lost in it … let's drop those two … a flight in a hot air balloon … what if one of them fell out? … and there aren't any hot air ballons in Nodd … get one over from Knotso … not so easy … an extra special dinner … yes, a feast … Chef Aygradouce would help … yes, he's always complaining his talents aren't given free rein … no need for extra work – just special food … I think we've got it … all agreed … YES!"

"Well," said Bailiff left, "what we need now is a menu, so let's dream on that and meet again tomorrow."

*   *   *

The birthday celebration team met again at Horngates Tower the next day and, after a good lunch, reinstalled themselves in the comfy chairs in the lounge to continue their deliberations.

"We both had good dreams," started Bailiff Left, "but Right had the more useful one as regards our plans for the birthday feast itself – if I may so call it now – so over to you, Right."

"Yes," began Right, "you will know, I expect, that the Wyrd Woods are full of truffles, which can, as I expect you will also know, be used to flavour particularly delicious risottos. So, in my dream I was in the Woods and as I walked past a Boggart hole at the foot of an ancient sycamore tree, I could smell what must have been the most beautifully perfumed truffle that I have ever smelt. Instantly I thought that if you could obtain that truffle it would make a risotto that would be the star dish of any celebration meal. Alas, the Boggart was not in residence, so I could pursue the matter no further, and I duly woke up – but thus to Left's dream."

"And I was busy in my dream studying my toes for information about Boggarts, and what I learnt was that they are slippery little creatures – great shape-shifters and very deceitful. So if you find this Boggart who lives under a sycamore tree in Wyrd Woods and try to persuade him to part with his wonderful truffle, you must be on your guard."

"Okay," said Bruin, " shall we go and look for him on our way home, Karlo, and see whether he'll let us have this truffle?"

"Why not, and I'll be my most charming and persuasive – we'll see who can be slippery and deceitful!"

"Yes," said Bruin, though with a slightly sceptical tone to her voice. "So whereabouts in the Woods was this Boggart's hole, Right? Can you give us some directions, please?"

"Certainly, it's very easy to find. Go through the gap in the hedge that you went through to find Joy, but take the first path on the left – it will follow the line of that hedge. You'll see the sycamore tree about 250 meters along on the right hand side; you can't miss it because the hole is at the base of the tree and has been gnawed through the trunk up to about 30 centimetres from the ground and then down underground through the roots – it's an impressive piece of Boggart engineering!"

"That's great – thanks, Right. Well, we'd better be getting along, and if we are successful then the next stage will be to decide on the rest of the menu and the guest list."

*   *   *

Meanwhile, the Boggart in question was sitting just inside his hole and singing merrily.

> I'm such a happy Boggart,
> My name is Thirty-Three,
> And the most important Boggart
> In the whole wide world is me!
>
> And the only skill a Boggart needs,
> If he his hole should leave,
> Is not to practise gallant deeds
> But tell lies and deceive.

And if I'm not mistaken
There's two humans on the way,
Who'll fall for my good fakin'
And make me very gay.

And from this we can learn four things about
Boggarts: first, that they do not have names but
numbers; second, that they are terribly conceited;
third, as Bailiff Left said, that they are great liars
and deceivers; and fourth, that they are atrocious
poets.

Be all that as it may, however, he was quite
right about the imminent arrival of two humans
because just at that point the twins arrived.

Karlo immediately pretended to be surprised
and greeted the Boggart with exaggerated courtesy
and more than a little condescension.

"Well, good afternoon, Mr Boggart – my
goodness, what a splendid hole you have there.
Did you make that all by yourself?"

"Oh my goodness!" said Boggart Thirty-Three
to himself with glee. "We have a plum ripe for the
picking here!" And then, with an affected modesty
to match Karlo's, replied to the boy, "I did indeed,
and how good of you to speak so kindly of it,
young man."

Karlo got onto his hands and knees to peer
right down into the hole and as he did so sniffed

loudly, following this extravagant behaviour with, "my goodness, is that a truffle I smell?"

Bruin, meanwhile, was hugging Joy to try and hide the fact that she could hardly stop herself from bursting out laughing.

"It is indeed," replied the Boggart, "and I doubt you'll ever smell another so fine, even if you live (as indeed I hope you will, dear boy) to be a hundred."

"I doubt it, too," said Karlo, "and what a coincidence this is, because my sister and I happen to be looking for a truffle to make a risotto for our parents' fortieth birthday dinner on this coming 14th of July – our parents being, I might add, no less than the queen and king of our well-governed island of Nodd. Would you be willing to part with it for an appropriate exchange – say, perhaps, a sack of brussels sprouts?"

The Boggart smiled an enigmatic smile as he thought to himself, "a sack of sprouts – he must be joking! I can get as many sprouts as I want by just going into a field on any moonlit night!" But then he suddenly realised how he could turn this situation to his advantage and said aloud, "well, by another most extraordinary coincidence it is my birthday too on that day, and I was planning to celebrate it by treating myself to a risotto made from this very truffle that you speak of; however, I would consider it a most prodigious honour to make a gift of it to our noble and gracious king and queen for their royal celebrations. Please allow me to do so."

"This is most extremely generous of you," replied Karlo, "and we are more than happy to accept your gift – but" (and here he turned to Bruin and mouthed silently to her, "good grief, I hope this scrawny little rat of a creature isn't expecting an invitation in return …") "we hope you will understand that because this will be a royal family event you wouldn't be able to partake of the risotto yourself."

"Of course, of course," said the Boggart, "I understand perfectly – I humbly make a gift of it to you without preconditions." And again he smiled his enigmatic little smile. "Allow me to go and fetch it." And he disappeared into the hole.

"Gosh, that was easier than I thought it would be," said Karlo to his sister.

"Yes," replied Bruin. "But perhaps a little too easy – I can't help wondering if he is up to something." Joy whined quietly in agreement.

"Well I can't think what," said Karlo airily. "We've got the truffle and that's what we came for – let's not look a gift-Boggart in the mouth – ah, he's back."

And indeed he was, holding a truffle the size of a pineapple that nestled in a bed of fresh moss and was emitting an intoxicating perfume.

*   *   *

Bruin and Karlo slipped round the back of the palace to the kitchen entrance with their prize and presented it to Chef Aygradouce. He welcomed it with astonishment and joy, saying that he had never seen or smelt such an amazing truffle.

He told the twins what he had planned for the rest of the menu, and they then went to Karlo's room to draw up the guest list, which they had agreed would be kept as small as possible so that maximum attention could be devoted to the birthday couple and there would be a minimum chance of the surprise being spoilt by careless talk. Invitations were then written and the two set out with Joy to deliver them.

*   *   *

The day arrived and the guests were seated around the circular dining table in the state banqueting room of the palace. This table, like the Round Table of King Arthur, was designed to make sure that nobody looked more important than

126

anyone else. Nodd had no concept of any one inhabitant being more important than another – the king and queen were just two people with a job to do, and so were considered no more useful than a shepherd or a sailor.

Everyone was reading the menu and saying excitedly that Chef Aygradouce had excelled himself.

"Oh – look at these starters: mushrooms millefeuille, broccoli and feta cheese with fresh herbs, and then – my goodness, honey glazed roast carrots with pecan nuts! And with them, Domaine Fulginea, Chablis Grand Cru, 2020."

"And then it's truffle risotto served with avocado and butter beans with preserved orange, charred aubergines with lemony yoghurt."

"And this one sounds lovely – saffron roasted courgettes and tomatoes."

"And with my favourite wine - Dogs of Knotso, Shiraz, 2019!"

"But there is still all this to come for dessert – chocolate iced yoghurt, lime cheesecake with pineapple purée topping, or summer fruits ice-cream."

"With our best dessert wine, Isle of Nodd, Horngates, Sauterne, 1998 – that's superb!"

"My toenails, I can't wait to get started!"

*   *   *

Once the feast was over and the guests had gone Bruin, Karlo and Joy headed for the kitchen to thank Chef Aygradouce for all the hard work and imagination that he had put into creating such a splendid banquet. Just as they entered the kitchen area, however, Joy ran into a side room whining menacingly. The twins followed her and to their astonishment found the Boggart sitting at a table, scoffing with obvious delight something that smelled suspiciously like truffle risotto.

"What on earth are you doing here?" cried Bruin.

The Boggart paused, looked up at them and said. "Just eating my share."

"What share?" responded Bruin, now more puzzled than angry. "You gave us the truffle – the whole truffle, without preconditions – remember?"

"Ah," said the Boggart, " but I kept a little corner for myself that I didn't tell you about – just a little corner, and now I've come to enjoy it."

Bruin and Karlo looked at one another and suddenly burst out laughing.

"Well," said Karlo, "I think we have to hand it to you. You really are the great deceiver! Enjoy the rest of your meal!"

And they turned to go, but as they did so the Boggart called them back. "Just hold on a second – I have something else to show you."

He shimmered slightly, and a split-second later standing there before them, to their great astonishment, was none other than Bailiff Left!

"Yes, I am indeed the great deceiver ..." she said with a smile, "... but don't give the game away!"

Bruin in Shadowland

Bruin walked briskly in the soft blue air of dawn, along the path that led to Horngates Tower. She was on her way to having breakfast with the Bailiffs. Would there be kedgeree, she wondered, made as it should be, with kippers and a touch of spice, or perhaps scrambled eggs with avocado pear, fresh peaches with honey and yogurt, toasted muffins and marmalade, and ginseng tea? The Bailiffs always put on a good breakfast spread, she mused, with eager anticipation.

Then something tugged at her mind from the left. But when she turned to see what it was she realised that it was something that wasn't, and to her surprise it was Karlo who wasn't.

"I was sure he was with me when we left the palace," she thought. "Where can he have gone? Where has Karlo gone …" she said aloud, looking behind her for Joy – but Joy, too, was not there.

Now she was really worried because Joy never left her side without a gentle howl of explanation.

"Maybe the Bailiff's will know where they are," thought Bruin, and she walked on towards

Horngates Tower.

The air began to turn a darker blue, then blueish-grey, and finally became a clammy and darkly grey cloud, which wrapped itself around her and hid the fresh morning world from her eyes.

*   *   *

As she walked through the gateway to the Bailiff's' Tower, Bruin had a sudden, disturbing sensation that something else was not quite right. She paused, and her eyes were drawn to the two large, curved Brachyderm tusks that formed the archway above her. She looked closely at them.

"That's very odd," she thought. "These tusks aren't pitted like they usually are – they're streaked with fine dark lines … Oh! This isn't bone – it's ivory!"

Being a true child of Nodd, Bruin realised immediately what this meant – that the dreams which passed though this gateway to the Bailiffs in Horngates Tower would not be true dreams, because true dreams will pass only through gateways made of bone, and dreams that pass through an ivory gateway are false.

She walked on down the path towards the front door of the tower, deep in thought, and, as she did so, a dark cloud drifted over her mind and cut her off from the world around her.

*   *   *

On reaching the front door Bruin pulled on the rope that rang the doorbell of Horngates Tower. It clattered like a sack of rusty tin cans being shaken violently by an angry gnome.

Bailiff Left appeared in the doorway.

"Oh, there you are, Bruin," she said without further ceremony. "We've been waiting for you. Breakfast is ready."

Bruin followed her, but instead of going through the first door off the hallway into the dining room where the breakfast would have been laid out the Bailiff carried on down a bare stone passageway that came out in a cave-like cellar where Bailiff Right was waiting for them. Then, to Bruin's astonishment – and indeed alarm – rather than going to stand beside her sister, Bailiff Left walked straight into her, merged with her, and turned round to face their guest, who saw now a grey, dour-faced figure with two good eyes, eyes that stared coldly at Bruin who would have turned and fled, were it not that she felt glued to the stone cellar floor.

"Welcome to Shadowland," said the grim caricature of her two erstwhile friends.

"Wh...wh...what is Shadowland?" stammered the terrified girl.
"Wh...wh...wh...where is Shadowland? Wh...wh...wh...wh...where am I?"

"Shadowland," said the creature, as though she were stating the merely obvious, "is where things are not – where the truth is disguise and misdirection."

"You mean where things are not what they seem to be?" asked Bruin, some of her natural confidence returning.

"If that's what you want it to mean," said the figure, "yes!"

"I want it to mean what it does mean," persisted Bruin.

"Well," came the reply, "you're in the wrong place for that. We would suggest that you turn your mind inside out if you want to understand what is going on here, because there are many different ways to speak falsely. The truth told in disguise or indirectly is just one. And of course, even what we have just said might be no more than disguise and misdirection."

This tangle of contradictions made Bruin feel faintly sick and faint. The air went grey, folded around the now singular Bailiff, and hid her from sight.

Bruin was back home, but the palace was deserted. She called for Joy but to no avail – not even the echo of a welcome-home howl. She went through all the downstairs rooms, but there was not so much as a single cat snoozing on a chair in the big audience room.

She tried Karlo's room upstairs, and that was as empty as a summer-holiday classroom.

She went into the garden. A lone blue lizard stared briefly at her from a black stone in the rock terrace, then flashed into invisibility like a streak of lightning, disappearing beneath something that was lying on the ground just in front of the rock terrace.

Bruin went over to look at it. What she found was a carved stone cupidon dressed incongruously in one of her old party frocks which she recognised as the one she wore for her tenth birthday party, just over a year ago. The cupidon's stone wings were broken underneath it, and its stone bow lay beside it on the grass in two pieces. Everything suggested that it had been hurled from the now empty pedestal at the top of the terrace.

The statuette stared up at her with a seemingly mocking grin – and winked one of its stone eyes.

A darkling shadow unfolded from the sky and covered Bruin and the garden.

*   *   *

As the shadow cleared Bruin found herself outside Wyrd Woods looking at the narrow, ragged gap in the hedge that she went through when she first met Joy.

She walked over to the gap and found, lying on the top of the hedge on her left, a stone arrow nearly a metre long with a heart-shaped point as sharp as a razor. It was pointing into the woods.

"What on earth – or who on earth – could shoot that?" she wondered. "Is there a stone bow somewhere that it belongs to, with a stone bowstring?"

She stared intently at the perplexing object which seemed to be struggling to tell her something. Suddenly, what the Bailiffs had said about truth as disguise and the broken stone bow of the cupidon in the palace garden came together in her mind, and immediately she saw the arrow for what it was.

"This is a puzzle," she thought, "and there's a piece missing, and this clue might lead me to it …"

She eased herself through the gap in the

hedge and headed for where she had met Joy in the glade of butterflies.

The butterflies had gone, and Joy, of course, was no longer there, but as she approached the spot where the wolf had been sitting she spied what she was looking for – a stone heart, about the size of a dinner plate, broken in two. And between the two halves of the stone heart a pool of thick, dark red liquid puddled the floor of pine cones that it was lying on.

"… and this is the piece," she thought with satisfaction, "that solves this puzzle of disguise and misdirection."

A light mist descended on the glade like a cloud of fluttering butterflies.

*   *   *

Drring drring! Drring drring! Drring drrring!

Bruin woke up, rolled over onto her back and stretched out her arms towards the braying alarm clock to switch it off. Almost immediately she felt a soft, damp nose nuzzling her left ear. She wrapped her arm around the wolf and pulled her closer.

"I've had a most interesting night of dreaming," she told the animal, "and after breakfast we are going to find out if I've understood correctly what it meant."

Joy whined appreciatively – this sounded promisingly as though a walk was going to be the order of the day.

Bruin got washed, then dressed for breakfast (her parents insisted that certain standards were maintained regarding meal times) and she and Joy went downstairs to join the rest of the family. On the sideboard she noticed with pleasure – not to mention with some interest – that Chef Aygradouce had prepared for the family kedgeree, made, as it should be, with kippers and a touch of spice, scrambled eggs, with a dish of sliced avocados beside the chafing dish which was keeping the eggs warm, fresh peach halves, honey, yogurt, muffins for toasting, marmalade, coffee and a variety of teas which included ginseng.

She helped herself to some kedgeree, surreptitiously concealing under her plate a muffin which, when she sat down, found its way into the wolf's open mouth.

"Well, Bruin," said her father, tactfully ignoring the wolf chomping on a filched muffin, "what have you got planned for this warm summer's day?"

"I think a walk to the Wyrd Woods this morning, and then perhaps a visit to the Bailiffs for lunch," replied Bruin.

"Oh – not the Wyrd Woods!" said Karlo. "I'm not coming with you if you're going there."

"That's okay," replied his sister. "I knew you wouldn't."

Karlo looked at her quizzically, but just grunted and got on with eating his cornflakes.

*   *   *

Bruin walked along Horngates Lane with Joy happily trotting beside her. The Wyrd Woods were just off this lane, about halfway to Horngates Tower. When they came into sight Bruin paused and looked keenly across the field that lay between her and the woods.

"No – a little further," she decided, and walked on.

At the next pause she said to Joy, "Here we are!" And the wolf, who also recognised where they were, gave a brief, quiet whine of agreement.

They slipped through the post and rail fence and headed across the grass to the narrow opening in the hedge. Here, lying on the top of the left hand side of the gap Bruin found the first object that she had expected to find – a small metal arrow with a very sharp, heart-shaped head and fine golden fletchings. It pointed towards the butterfly glade inside the woods.

She looked carefully at the arrow, but did not pick it up. She knew that it was just a clue – literally a pointer – and must not be disturbed, because if it was she might lose her way. What mattered was what it pointed to, so she and Joy pushed through the gap and on towards the butterfly glade.

*   *   *

Meanwhile, down at the Port of Nodd, a family was disembarking from a ship that had brought them back home from the neighbouring island of Knotso. The parents, Lyvva and Escalus Vayse, the Treasurers of Nodd, had been lent by Clotilde and Clovis to the King and Queen of Knotso for a year to help them sort out the finances of the island which had got into a parlous state after pirates had stolen all the gold in their treasury one stormy night.

First off the ship was their son, Severin, eager to get to the palace to see his favourite playmates, Bruin and Karlo, and who, of course, he had not seen for a year. But his parents were taking their time making arrangements with the sailors for the transport of their luggage, of which there was a considerable heap.

"Come on dad!" called Severin eagerly.

"Let's get a move on!"

"All in good time," replied his father – then added with a smile, "But you go ahead if you're so keen to see your friend."

"Friends!" said Severin emphatically, but blushing as he did so. And he set off on his own towards the palace at a brisk pace.

*   *   *

Bruin went to the spot where Joy was sitting when she found the wolf, and began examining the ground carefully, brushing away some of the dried leaves and twigs. Joy, however, stopped a few metres short of that spot, and started whining in a "come over here" sort of way that made Bruin take notice of her.

When Bruin reached her, Joy rolled over on to her back and started pedalling the air with her front paws, just as she had when Bruin and Karlo had first stroked her. As she did so she brushed her paw against Bruin's neck and Bruin distinctly felt a slight tug, as though the paw had momentarily caught in something. Joy then jumped back onto her legs, pushed her nose into the leaves and Bruin saw a flash of crimson light. She pounced and there it was in her hand – the tiny Cupid's Heart made of dark red Venetian glass on a delicate gold chain that she had been given on her tenth birthday. She had lost it all too soon after it had been given to her, but she never knew when or where.

She picked it up and kissed it gently, then stared intently at it, particularly at the mysterious tiny slot in the centre: :That is the last missing bit of the puzzle," she thought to herself, "and the last thing I have to find."

"Come on, Joy, let's go to see the Bailiffs – it's time for lunch."

" Uuoooowwwwwwww!" replied Joy, who always looked forward to lunch at Horngates Tower because she was given extra-special treats by her friends Bailiff Left and Bailiff Right.

*　　*　　*

By the time Severin arrived at the palace he was almost running. He threw himself at the main door and rang the entry bell, and then stood by the front door, hopping up and down with excitement. The door was opened by Karlo, who gasped with astonishment and then took Severin in his arms and hugged him. The new arrival, gasping for breath, disentangled himself from his old friend, muttered appropriate enquiries about how he was, had the Summer holidays been good so far, had

141

Karlo had any good dreams etc. etc. … and could he come in to see the rest of the family.

"Yes, yes, of course!" was the welcome reply. "We're just about to have lunch so come in and join us!"

Severin almost jumped across the threshold, and throwing his arm around Karlo's shoulder dragged him towards the dining room. "Terrific! I'm famished!" he exclaimed, by way of excuse for his unmannerly haste.

The two friends tumbled into the dining room, and Severin looked eagerly round the table and into every corner, but after thoroughly scouring the room his face fell – someone was missing!

*   *   *

Bruin and Joy arrived at Horngates Tower and rang the doorbell, which sang its accustomed melodious tune. Bailiff Left opened the door and welcomed them in.

"Well, well, well," she said with a smile, "by a strange coincidence you two are just in time for lunch!"

After the meal Bruin told the Baliffs about her dream of being in Shadowland, her consequential interpretation of it, the recovery of her Cupid's Heart necklace, and that she was now looking for the missing piece that she believed should have been in that curious slot in the centre.

"Now," said Bailiff Right, "we happened to be in that dream as well last night, so we know what you're looking for."

"And what's more," added Bailiff Left with a knowing wink, "I think I know why you are looking for it. Could that be because it was given to you by a special friend?"

Bruin blushed a blush as red as the Cupid's Heart.

"Yes," she whispered.

"So would you be interested to learn, said the Bailiff, looking hard at her left big toe, "that I can see this same special friend at this very moment having lunch with your family in the palace?"

Bruin leapt up, flustered and excited at the same time.

"May I go, please, Bailiffs …. would you mind … I know I'm being very rude but …"

"Of course, of course," said Bailiff Right, chuckling quietly. "We understand perfectly. Off you go, the pair of you!"

Bruin and the wolf ran to the door and out through the archway of horn.

* * *

Severin was half way along Horngates Lane hurrying towards the Bailiff's Tower, with a breathless Karlo trying to keep up behind him.

Bruin was halfway along Horngates Lane hurrying towards the palace, with Joy loping happily alongside her.

They saw one another at the same precious instant and ran even faster to meet up at exactly the central point of the lane.

"Hello!" …"Hello!" was breathlessly exchanged and they stood looking at one another for a full ten seconds in astonished, bewildered uncertainty. At last Bruin put out her hand, Severin put out his, and they met in a heartfelt grasp.

"I've got something for you, Bruin," gasped Severin. "A small present …"

"I know, Severin," gasped Bruin, "and I know what it is – it's the last piece of a puzzle! Look – I have my part here – your tenth birthday present to me. I lost it nearly a year ago, and found it again today – look!"

And she took the Cupid's Heart necklace out of her dress pocket and showed it to Severin. He looked at it with delight, remembering with pleasure how he had bought it in a second-hand shop down by the port, and had been puzzled by the tiny slot in the middle of the heart. He then took out of his pocket a small wooden casket that just fitted in the palm of his hand.

"I found this," he said, "in the same shop where I bought the necklace – it was when we were waiting for the boat to take us across to Knotso, and I've kept it carefully all the year we were away."

He opened the little casket, and gently removed a tiny golden arrow with a red heart-shaped point.

Taking Bruin's hand in his, he held the Cupid's Heart between them and pushed the little arrow through the slot.

"See," he said quietly, "how one heart can transfix another."

And as they embraced two real, fast-beating hearts melted, and became one.

Printed in Dunstable, United Kingdom

73127760R00087